Father's Day

Father's Day

◆

Encounters with Everyday Life

Raphael Badagliacca

For Harriet,

An accomplished writer
but an even
greater person.

Please enjoy
these stories
half as much
as I enjoy your
presence.

Raphael Badagliacca

iUniverse, Inc.

New York Lincoln Shanghai

Father's Day
Encounters with Everyday Life

Copyright © 2007 by Raphael Badagliacca

iUniverse books may be ordered through booksellers or by contacting:

iUniverse
2021 Pine Lake Road, Suite 100
Lincoln, NE 68512
www.iuniverse.com
1-800-Authors (1-800-288-4677)

ISBN: 978-0-595-44059-7 (pbk)
ISBN: 978-0-595-88382-0 (ebk)

Printed in the United States of America

for my parents,
may this book find them

Contents

Acknowledgement

Special thanks to Ann Rubin for editorial suggestions, and to my wife and children for their understanding and support.

For more information about this book, or to share comments on the stories with other readers, visit www.fathersdaybook.com.

Bedtime Story

The baby's crying had just turned to sobbing. He was shouting "Mommy!" in a plaintive, pathetic voice. He had been doing it for half an hour.

My wife was in tears, too. We were behind the closed door of our room lying on the bed. I was looking into her face, reminding her, "We can't go!" She looked away from me.

"Remember the doctor's advice?" I said. "We've been doing it all wrong."

For the first year of his life we went to him as soon as he made the slightest sound. My wife had anticipatory hearing. She could hear sounds before they happened. "He's about to cry," she would announce, and jump off the bed and into the darkness.

We made the excuse that at first he didn't have his own room, and that we were concerned about the neighbors. Our apartment building suffered from vertical noise, the cause of serious disagreements among the tenants.

But the facts were that no one had ever said the slightest thing to us about the crying. We were the ones it bothered, because we couldn't bear to think that there was something he needed that we weren't giving him.

"Mommy!"

By looking at her I knew one more "Mommy" would break the dam.

"He's got his own room, now," I said, trying to sound reasonable. "He's got to learn how to fall asleep on his own. "The doctor said …"

"Did you ask the doctor about his own baby!" she asked. "Well, he does the same thing we've been doing," she said. "He doesn't follow his own theories when it's *his* baby crying."

1

"Mommy! MOMMY!"

He was reaching a new level of desperation and so was she. In my mind, I saw him imprisoned in his crib, holding onto the bars, falsely accused. This was his one call for justice, and we refused to answer it. His own parents.

"Mommy!"

She looked at me pleadingly, but much as I would have liked to trash the experiment, I held my ground. "We can't go," I said.

And then he just stopped. The same look of fear came over both of our faces, the same thought entered both of our heads. Had he stopped breathing entirely? Had he collapsed in despair?

We paused and listened. We wanted to hear something—whimpering, rustling—anything to tell us he had given up the fight but would live to take it up another day. We were like the citizens in a western begging for some sign as the gun smoke cleared that our hero still stood.

And then it happened.

"Daddy!"

I looked at my wife.

"Daddy!"

Hearing it gave me a peculiar feeling—pleasant and painful at once.

"Daddy!"

"Daddy!"

And then I heard myself say, "I've gotta go … I've never been called before."

"Daddy!"

So I walked to his room in a trance-like state. He was my son and he needed me. Sure it had taken him awhile to realize it. After all, he saw so much more of Mommy. Mommy fed him and clothed him and bathed him. Mommy picked him up when he fell, and Mommy was there most of the time.

But now he needed Daddy, and Daddy was not going to let him down. What was one night in a lifetime of nights? He could learn to fall asleep on his own tomorrow.

The room was dimly lit. He was standing exactly as I thought he would be, with his hands on the bars. He was worn and tear-stained and toughened by the ordeal. I walked towards him to make amends, to reach down as his father and lift him out of his despair.

He said two words: "Get Mommy!"

The Suitcase

When you become a parent, everything changes, even what you carry.

One day, my wife announced that she was taking our new baby boy to see my parents. I had two very important presentations that day, so important that I bought a new suit for the occasion—a dark tropical wool with a subtle pinstripe. I'm not in the least bit superstitious, but twice before I'd done very well while wearing a red tie, so I purchased three ties with red in them to go along with the suit. I was selecting the one that looked the luckiest as my wife outlined the day's arrangements. She would take the car and I would join them later by train.

My day went very well. By early afternoon, I was back in the office, feeling sure I had the beginnings of two new, large accounts. With that kind of success, I was ready to call it a day when the phone rang. It was my wife. She had forgotten my son's Winnie-the-Pooh suitcase, full of baby things that she needed. Would I mind stopping by the apartment to get it on my way to the train?

"No problem," I said, even though the apartment and the train were in two entirely different directions. I straightened the papers on my desk and left for the day. At the apartment, I exchanged my polished leather briefcase for the baby's suitcase. It was mostly white, with yellow and red trim. The characters from the story cavorted across the case—Tigger and Piglet and Winnie himself. I remembered the part in the book about how Tigger and Winnie were such good friends that when they wanted to see each other they both got the thought at the same time and met at a place in the forest they know so well.

It was a spring day. I left the house without an overcoat.

I descended into the subway. I stood on the platform, a rising executive wearing an elegant, new suit and holding his Winnie-the-Pooh suitcase.

When the train arrived the doors shot open, and I shot into a seat, with the suitcase between my feet. The subway cars were always so full of peculiarities—from beggars without legs to religious fanatics delivering fiery sermons—that my little oddity didn't even register.

After the subway ride, I swung through the turnstiles at Penn Station and took my spot next to hundreds of commuters, waiting for the board to light up with the arrival of my train.

Once on the train, I took the double seat at the front facing another double seat. There is only one pair of seats like this in each car. I put the suitcase next to me. A young woman took the seat across from me. She immediately took a report of some kind from her briefcase and began to study it.

As the train moved through the tunnel, I studied her reflection in the blackened glass. She had those big screen looks buttoned up in a very corporate style. In one of those Fifties movies, she would have inherited the business from her father, been dismissed as a mere woman by the Board of Directors, and proved herself by the end of the film to be more fiercely competitive than any of them. Along the way, she would meet and fall in love with the leading man who wore a suit remarkably like the one I had on today.

She was quite beautiful. And that her business suit revealed nothing made her even more enticing. But wait a minute. My wife was just as beautiful, and just as capable. And besides, this was the happiest time of my life, now that we had our little boy. Maybe they'd even meet me at the train station. I resolved to conquer this thing that always made you feel you were losing a little part of your life if beauty moved in and out of it and you did nothing about it. I would continue to enjoy the movie in the glass, but I determined I did not have to say anything.

Then she spoke to me.

She cleared her throat slightly, so I turned to look at her.

She looked at me and then at my Winnie-the-Pooh suitcase, which I was now clutching for some reason.

Then very carefully and very slowly, she said with her perfect lips:

"Are you running away from home?"

Baby Steps

We never really thought of you as a baby. Right from the start, you seemed to understand what we were saying, even what we were thinking.

"This baby cries real tears," your grandmother said, "real, wet tears." You also had a real laugh, one of the happiest sounds I ever heard.

You put those real tears to good use in the first months of your life. I walked for miles with you in the wee hours. We saw so much of the 24-hour news channel that we became experts in the year of your birth. Terrible things happened. People fought with stones and knives and machine guns in faraway places. One night, two men were dragged from a car and murdered by a mob. The world was in turmoil, as always, but with your constant crying in the background those scenes finally seemed to find the accompaniment they deserved.

I tried everything to comfort you. I sang songs. I told stories.

I told you about the boy and the mysterious thing he could feel but not see. The way you looked at me, I felt sure you understood every word, saw the leaves moving as I described them, knew the boy was you, and the mysterious, invisible thing—the wind.

Sometimes I told the story about the walk I took with my sister every Saturday morning.

One night your grandparents showed us steps they had learned at an adult class in ballroom dancing. Excited and happy, they announced that your aunt and I would be taking classes from the same teacher. I wasn't sure I liked the idea.

We learned the cha-cha, the foxtrot, the tango, the waltz … Each had its own special feeling and structure. Those lessons taught me the difference between getting something almost right and getting it exactly right. When it's right, it feels effortless, like playing—something you do very well.

Every week for two full years, we walked to the teacher's house. We saw the tree in her front yard sprout buds and drop leaves, and we saw it bare against the winter sky.

I broke the spell. I explained to Mom and Dad that I could no longer attend because I had joined the high school track team. We had Saturday practices. The coach had his own dances to teach—the quarter mile, the 220-yard dash, the distance medley.

New worlds opened up. I met girls and went to dances, but never a dance where I could use one of the steps I had learned.

Dancing had become something different. As people moved with improvised motions, I would walk around the edge of the room—full of knowledge that had somehow become useless. No one wanted to tango. No band played the waltz, or the rumba.

Eventually, I did join in. But I never stopped thinking, how useless the waltz. Why did I spend so many mornings learning it against my will?

Whenever I finished this story, I picked up little you, so little, and held you the proper distance from me, and let the music come humming out of my mouth—one-two-three, one-two-three, one-two-three—and as I heard the incessant crying quiet to a miraculous whimper and then stop, I knew why I had learned the waltz.

Fire Island

Fire Island, summer haven off the coast of Long Island, owes its name to a typographical error. As the story goes, an early cartographer set out to label, rather unimaginatively, a group of *Five Islands*, but his handwritten *v* looked like an *r*, and the name stuck. For ten consecutive years, I spent summer weekends and vacation weeks on this island, in the family communities of Fair Harbor and then Seaview. I was there as a single person, a married person, and eventually, a parent.

The island is well known for its white beaches, its astonishing sunsets which residents meet on the docks, drinks in hand, to toast, applauding as the sun sinks into the horizon, its famous lighthouse, its wildlife, and, on occasion, its horrific, life-threatening weather. But Fire Island's uniqueness lies in what it does not have.

No cars. No sight, no sound, no smell of automobiles. The only way onto or off of the island is by water. Ferries run on schedules between the mainland and the towns. The importance of this difference cannot be exaggerated. It is felt, hours and sometimes days before it is understood, as a general sense of well-being and peacefulness with no identifiable cause. It is a subtle and effective introduction to a past in which we did not live, but from which we come, on equal footing with nature and each other, because we only have our feet to take us there.

It was Monday morning, after a week's vacation on the island. I had boarded the ferry and driven the two hours back to New York City and the modern world, leaving the family to enjoy another week. I would join them again on Friday. My wife's aunt and uncle from Seattle, with their two children, were visiting. I was at my desk, arranging the workday, when the telephone rang.

It was my father-in-law. "I want you to know," he said, "that the baby's alright."

This was an ominous phone call. He was not on the island with the baby, my two-year old son, which meant that someone had called him and he was calling to tell me something that he was not saying.

"What's wrong?" I said.

"Nothing's really wrong," he said unconvincingly. And then he said: "The baby severed his finger."

I must have shut my eyes. I know I saw black. I ran down the two flights of stairs, juggling the details of the story as they had been given to me, and out to the car. I headed back in the direction from which I had just come.

Just as she had on several other mornings, my wife dropped the baby off in the morning at a friend's house, where a young woman studying for a master's degree in child-care looked after three children for a few hours. Not once on any of these days had my wife returned to check on the baby, but for some reason on this morning, she turned around and walked back after buying the morning newspaper. Not ten minutes had passed.

She came back to find blood in the entrance and seemingly everywhere. The baby was huddled into the corner of the room. He wasn't crying; he was in shock, holding his hand against his body. The baby-sitter was also in shock, stone silent, unable to move. The other two children were wailing loudly.

My wife rushed to the baby, who now began to cry, as if her presence had given him permission. The index finger on his left hand, cleanly cut, was hanging, attached only by a layer of skin. Even now, years later, I cringe when I imagine his finger in the small space near the hinge on the metal door as it's slammed shut.

In her fifth month of pregnancy, she picked him up and ran out of the house and down the block in the direction of the doctor's office. She was met on the way by the neighbor in whose house the destruction had taken place. The neighbor left two full bags of groceries in the middle of the sidewalk as they now ran together towards the doctor.

The doctor's office looked like just another summer house, except that the nurse, who was also the receptionist, had a desk. The desk was vacant. The neighbor knocked on the inner door. The doctor was sitting across from an elderly patient.

"We have an emergency," she said.

"I'm with a patient," the doctor said.

"It's a child. It's an emergency," the neighbor said. She was a slight woman, but she seemed ready to lift the doctor out of his seat and take him to the wounded boy if he did not willingly open his door.

The doctor seemed flustered. He failed at making a successful tourniquet. He was not used to cases like this one. Most days, he consulted on how to treat poison ivy and removed large splinters that bare feet picked up from the wooden walkways. The best thing he did was to alert the helicopter from the mainland, which would meet them on the softball field.

From my car, I called my son's pediatrician to let him know what had happened. Although I had not spoken to my wife, I now knew the name of the hospital where they planned to take him. People didn't have cell phones as they do now. I set up a conference call on my car phone between the pediatrician and the hospital staff, but the voices were too faint for them to hear each other, so I made sure everyone had everyone else's number, and I got out of the conversation.

Now, silence. I had a long ride ahead of me, but it seemed wrong to put on music, or talk radio, or anything that might create distraction. I was powerless. I fell into a kind of parental thinking in the extreme: maybe if I paid no attention to my own needs, things would work out for him. I kept imagining what it would be like to have a child with only nine fingers. How many times would we have to explain how it had happened? What effect would it have on his future? I drove to the hospital in complete silence.

On the way to the softball field, they ran into my wife's aunt on her way to the beach. She joined the group. They waited for endless minutes on the field, looking skyward, listening for the sound of the rotor blades. Meanwhile, the helicopter was landing on the wrong softball field, in another town.

It took another fifteen minutes before this confusion was cleared up. Every minute that passed created more anxiety because anyone who knew how completely detached the finger was wondered how significant a factor time would be. As the helicopter appeared in the sky, the volunteer firemen who had by now also joined the group moved the growing crowd off the field to make room for the landing.

The EMS staff placed the baby on a stretcher and secured it within the helicopter. My wife wanted her aunt to accompany her. They had to make a decision about how many people could ride. Before my wife's aunt boarded, an EMS staffer loudly asked her over his megaphone what she weighed. She is by no means an overweight woman or a comedian, but she hesitated, and asked: "Do I have to tell?" Despite the tenseness of the moment, the crowd laughed.

More than the sight of the blood, more than the sound of his crying, more than the fear in his eyes, what struck my wife hardest, and made her break down, was the voice over the helicopter radio asking for confirmation that the *amputee* was aboard the craft and on the way to the hospital.

I took a spot in the visitor's parking lot at the hospital. Even though I felt like running, I walked to the entrance, as if by containing myself I would help contain the outcome, increasing the chances that it would be positive. I found them all in a wide, open room, both sets of grandparents, my sister, my brother-in-law, my wife's aunt, still in her bathing suit, and my wife, wearing her robe and pajamas, seated like the mother in Michelangelo's sculpture, *la pieta*, with our son stretched across her, asleep, his hand and arm bandaged. Utter exhaustion everywhere.

The family went to my sister's house, nearest to the hospital. I drove my wife's aunt back to the ferry that would take her back across to Fire Island. Her week-long vacation had begun with a bang. She was cold in her bathing suit. I gave her a blanket we kept in the car.

I drove back to my sister's house. On the way, I stopped at a department store and bought as many ninja turtles and power rangers as I could find, out of gratefulness for the preliminary report that everything would be fine, that, thanks to a skilled micro-surgeon, everyone's speedy action, and my wife's instincts, he would have the full use of his finger as if nothing had ever happened.

When I arrived at my sister's house, I found him playing with the kids out front, riding a tricycle with one hand, the enormous bandage extending outwards. He was laughing and having a good time. In the years to come, he wouldn't remember anything about this day, except that he had had a helicopter ride.

Like someone thrown off a horse, we climbed right back on, returning to the summer house for the last week of the season. On Sunday, I walked down to the softball field for the last game of the year. The summer was ending all around us. I put my glove on the edge of the stands, and stretched in preparation for the game. There were two women sitting there.

"Did you hear about the hospital helicopter?" one asked. "It landed right there."

"What happened?" the other woman said.

"A little kid got bit by a dog."

The Question

Our three-year old son was sitting in the kitchen of our New York City apartment with his mother and his aunt. They were trying to get him to say that he knew they were sisters.

"Baby, Mommy and Aunt Cindy are what? We're both what? We're both ..."

"Girls," he answered.

"You're right, we're both girls," my wife said. "But what else are we? We're both ..."

He was sitting at the table like one of the grownups, in a chair high enough for him to rest his elbows on the checkered tablecloth.

"We're both what?"

They looked remarkably alike. Even though Cindy was younger and taller, they were taken for each other all the time. Now they both held their heads tilted at the identical angle, anticipating his answer.

"Women," he said.

Aunt Cindy laughed. "You're a smart boy," she said.

He was getting impatient with the game, but my wife persisted. "You're right again, baby, but what else are we? We're girls and we're women, but what else are Aunt Cindy and I? We're ..."

Now he took his time. He looked at them. They had the same coloring and facial structure. My wife had her hair up, while Cindy's reached her shoulders. Cindy's hair was slightly darker, but it was very nearly the same color.

"What are we, baby?" my wife repeated.

For a long moment, he searched their faces for the answer, put his lips together very deliberately, and then said, "Humans."

Their laughter was uncontrollable. My wife stood up and leaned against the refrigerator, holding her side, while Cindy's laughter dissolved into tears. The laughter went on for about two minutes. When they had settled down, they returned to the interrogation.

"You are the smartest boy I know," my wife said. "But what are Aunt Cindy and I? It's true that we're *girls* and it's true that we're *women*, and it's true that we're *humans*." They both laughed again. "But what else are we? When you look at Cindy and me you know that we are what?"

He was out of answers, but he also wanted to please them. He looked at each of them again for a long moment. Then he looked down at the tablecloth as if the answer was hidden in the checkerboard pattern. Then he looked back at them together, at their hair and eyes and hands, and their eyes again.

He said, "Mammals."

First Communion

Entering the church building, I felt the same way I had unpacking the old toy trains, as if raising a child had given me passage back into my own childhood.

I signed in the space next to the words: "Teacher's Assistant." I was happy to learn that the teacher was an actual teacher of children in real life. I expected my duties as assistant to consist of handing out the pencils and helping to straighten the desks.

She was an attractive, shapely, young woman, exactly the kind of teacher I would have fallen for if I were a second-grader. She had a firm, friendly approach when addressing the entire class, but when an individual student came forward she looked right into his face unwaveringly, making him feel as if he were the only one in the universe.

She didn't show up for the third class. The nun in charge of the program handed me a note to say that a personal emergency would leave me on my own today.

To understand what happens next, best turn to the nature channel: On the Serengeti, the jackals sense the presence of a lone wildebeest, even before they see him. They descend upon him in what the casual observer might call frenzy, but is actually a calculated, almost choreographed approach to the prey. All twenty-two, no, twenty-one of twenty-two strike at once.

Only the deaf boy sitting in the front row did not join the mayhem. Many minutes passed before I got the situation under control by making a few threateningly loud sounds. I also glanced at the clock to check out exactly how many more minutes would have to pass before the parents came to my rescue. I decided that not much teaching would take place today. I would be content to get them to repeat back to me why they were there in the class. After many amusing answers, I got what I wanted: to prepare for our first communion. This was enough progress for me in my substitute role.

The next week when I arrived there was a folded note for me on the desk. I read it slowly and the emotions it made me feel must have been showing on my face because when I lowered the piece of paper, I saw the deaf boy standing a few yards away looking at me sympathetically. The note simply said that she would not be returning, and that the class was mine to teach for the rest of the schedule.

It is wrong to show fear to an opponent who outnumbers you. I must have failed to follow that guideline, because, once again, the room started to rock. Did they sense that my appearance alone two weeks in a row meant that I now belonged to them? I battled through the hour. I did not stick as closely to the text as the real teacher, who no doubt had years of classroom preparation behind her. But I made it through despite the loud noise, the persistent whispering, the items thrown back and forth and the wisecracks. Before the class ended, I got them to repeat once again why they were there, for my own benefit as well as theirs. Silently, I built a most-wanted list.

It may have been with this list in my mind that I quizzed the nun in charge when she came by at the end of the class. At her request, I came out to the hallway with her.

"How is it going?" she asked. I checked for a hearing aid.

"Sister," I said. "Can I re-arrange the children in their chairs? I'd like to make three sections—Hell, Purgatory, and Heaven."

She started laughing and coughing. It lasted for an uncomfortably long time, what seemed like five minutes.

"No, you can't," she said, when she had collected herself. "But I know what you mean," she added, walking away, down the hallway.

The boys and the girls posed different kinds of challenges. For the most part, the boys who cut up did it in impulsive, goofy ways. They gave me the impression that they expected to get caught and that getting caught was actually a badge of some kind. The girls were better planners. They were more patient, and you couldn't catch them at anything without eliciting the body language and the facial expression of a total innocent.

Gradually, things quieted down. I think we realized that we were all in a situation not completely of our own choosing and that we had to get through it together to get to the next place.

The deaf boy always sat in the same chair, right in front of me. Since he read lips, I became very aware of looking straight ahead at the class whenever I spoke. I also chose my words carefully, left out extra words, got right to the point of what I was saying, and for this new understanding of clarity and directness, I had him to thank.

We covered every lesson, although maybe not in the exact order they were presented in the book. I used my own examples, many of them drawn from the conflicts we experienced right in the classroom. I had to admit that I was proud of the children on at least one score: no matter how fiercely they battled me, never once had they shown the slightest impatience with the deaf boy, or, as far as I could tell, made him feel any more different than he already did. He always stood when he answered a question, and he did it by mouthing the way he thought the words should sound. If the lessons were not about this kind of generosity, then what were they about?

When the big day came, the boys all appeared in dark suits with their hair neatly brushed, and the girls in their white communion dresses. They looked like perfect angels, incapable of wrongdoing. As the organ music rose into the nave of the church, we stood together, students of the possibility of a state of grace, however fleeting.

Star Shower

I stood by myself on the porch and counted sixteen shooting stars. Then I went into the backyard where I found just as good a view, if not better, because there are fewer trees. From there, I noticed that the shower was taking place all over the sky. I went upstairs to see about my wife, but she was sleeping too peacefully to waken, even for a celestial event. I let Jack the dog out, but only on the leash, because I knew I wouldn't be able to shout so early in the morning to get him back. In his astonishment at this strange stroke of luck in the darkness, he bolted away from me and ran right up against the car, which set off the alarm. It took me about ten seconds to disable it. Instead of running away, he went to his usual spot under the tree and lay down, as if tethered. I thought, how mature he's become; he used to run away at every opportunity; see, things do change. I looked up and counted the shooting stars, which came at intervals, one at a time, like fireworks, except because they displayed horizontally, they seemed to be on urgent missions. Some of the meteor tails were tinged with color—green and pink. After I'd counted my 44th shooting star, certainly a lifetime quota, I went over to get Jack only to discover that his well-behaved form was actually part of a bush that looked like a dog lying down in the darkness. It took me an hour to collect him, and I needed the car, my jangling keys, and a long walk to do it. In the end, he showed up when he wanted to, in front of the house, and acted like we were just running into each other on the way to the train station; he had that "what's up?" look on his face. It was just enough astronomy and just enough earthly chaos to put me in my place in the universe.

Syzygy

Night in the town where we live is especially dark. This is because the streets are not electrified. Instead, we have gas lamps.

The gas lamps give the town a feeling of elegance, but they don't give much light. The combination of low light and uneven sidewalks has sent more than one new resident sprawling. The standing joke is that you need a miner's hat with a beacon to keep from falling. Many a pizza delivery boy has spent precious minutes hopelessly searching for the right house while the pie cooled off.

For a few hours on one evening, a celestial event changed all of this.

In our house, we had just moved into a new phase called adolescence. In this phase, the predictable becomes unpredictable. Speech is replaced by awkward silences. Gestures of affection, especially in public, are suddenly off limits. The worst thing a parent can do is attempt to say something funny in a car full of teenage friends. It will soon be made clear that as driver your job is to drive to the destination without saying a single word, like the man with the top hat in a hansom cab.

Parents experiencing adolescence undergo physical changes. They begin to feel old, so old that they can't remember their own adolescences. They're prone to exaggeration and wild mood swings. They begin to doubt themselves and ask if they are the only ones feeling these massive changes.

For me, one change symbolized everything—my son was ambivalent about having a catch. How many times had we taken out the ball and two gloves in his short life—two hundred, five hundred, a thousand?

I remember a variation where we tossed an orange in the kitchen, stealthily, underhandedly, because his mother had announced—no ball playing in the house!

How many times had he come to me with the question: "Wanna have a catch?" I always wanted to have a catch. Throwing a baseball was for me one of the most life-affirming acts on the globe. Each throw recognized our separateness; each catch confirmed our connection.

We threw softballs, hardballs, tennis balls, a cloth ball we called the crooked ball, even a frisbee on occasion. We kept track of our streaks—how many throws we could make without dropping the ball? He asked me to throw him hard grounders, and he responded with spectacular leaping throws to my first baseman's stance. He asked me to throw him high pop-ups, which I did the way my cousin had shown me many years ago, looking up and throwing overhand.

There may have been one or two or a dozen times in his life when I was too preoccupied to say, "Yes, I'll have a catch with you," and now I regret every one of them, but not as much as I regret the day I came to him and said, "Wanna have a catch?" and he answered me with: "That's alright," which in his new, relaxed lingo meant simply "No." I was devastated.

The dictionary defines *syzygy* as an event in which three or more celestial bodies are in perfect alignment. On one night in the recent past, the northeastern United States experienced a syzygy and our town, one of the darkest places in the universe, was flooded with light at 9:30PM.

Earlier in the evening, I had persuaded my son to come out at the appointed time to see something he might never see again. Once out, we did something it seemed as if we had not done since the mornings in New York City when I would bring him to pre-school. We went for a walk.

It only lasted five minutes, but it was full of a sense of discovery under that impossible light, just as it had been back then, when we ran from the two-headed monster drainpipes, avoided the cracks in the sidewalk, and jumped up from the street over each curb with both feet together.

We found ourselves back in front of the house. The same thought rushed to our lips: "Wanna have a catch?"

And so we did, adding a fourth celestial body to the perfect alignment of this evening—the orb traveling between us.

Another Moon

I can't remember the particulars. I just know it was another one of those days when the world seemed to be coming apart. It was coming apart in that way that made you believe it would never come together again. It made you feel that it had always been falling apart, even when you thought it was so close to coming together.

These were the kind of thoughts that immersed me when my daughter in her car seat began to ask me questions about the moon.

We were driving across a wide expanse, and to our left we could see a broken sky-line of hotels and office buildings. The moon was full and low in the sky. The sky was the darkest midnight blue, and the moon nearly white. As we traveled, it moved with us, ducking behind the buildings, and then re-appearing. This delighted my daughter endlessly.

She kept saying, "Where is the moon?"

Then, "There it is!"

She had appeared for us like the moon—our third child, a beautiful girl.

I couldn't get free of my thoughts. There seemed never to be enough of what was needed to move forward. It would be so much better if the situation were entirely hopeless. Then I could just walk away, but walk away to what? Did it have to be this way?

There was an endless restlessness about it all. You were staring wide-eyed at the future and there seemed to be no future. The arrears were always there, sucking you down. Nothing would ever change.

We were at the house. I didn't remember getting there. I didn't remember pulling up the driveway just a moment ago. The thoughts about not enough, the not enough-ness of everything was dragging me down. It would always be that way. Nothing would ever change. Miracles were for someone else.

As I lifted the baby out of the car, she put her head on my shoulder for a moment. Then she straightened up and pointed behind me.

She said: "Look Daddy, another moon!"

Aftermath

I asked the girls if they would like to go for ice cream, because it was the most normal thing I could think of to do. My daughter is six and her best friend is seven. They piled into the back seat of the car, as they would have on any other day and dutifully clipped on their seat belts for safety. Meanwhile the radio tried to get its hands around disaster with numbers.

There is safety in numbers. If you can measure it, isn't that the beginning of understanding? But the mayor had refused to speculate. He had said that we should expect an unimaginable number of deaths. But wasn't even one death unimaginable? Would not the grief of one family be infinite grief? And when you multiply it? The unimaginable magnitude of the thing had brought down the certainty of numbers with everything else.

The girls were chatting, as they would have any other day. There was the excitement of going someplace in their voices. They were two beautiful girls. Not just cute, but beautiful. In ten years, they would be breaking hearts—Miabelle and Isabel. "I hear two bells," I would say. It was our joke. "Miabelle and Isabel," they would shout back, in chorus. And then I would say, "I see two belles." And they would shout again: "Miabelle and Isabel." For now, the homonym would be my secret.

Even though we see the lighted New York City skyline on a clear night, we live in a small town. Because I am never home so early in the day, I observed the activity on our sidewalks like a tourist. There goes the electrician crossing the street. The landscaper's long vehicle is heading to the next job. So that's where the merchants do their banking. There was a constant moving of cars in and out of parking places.

Only the wording on the sign in front of the antique store gave away that there was a difference between a normal day last week and this week. Instead of the usual reminder that the owners bought and sold things of value, the letters had been re-arranged to say: "Noble Eagle Soar With Razored Talons."

The voices on the radio were telling us that planes of that type carry 10,000 gallons of fuel, that flames produced by such fuel reach 2,000 degrees, that buildings of that size contain 3 billion tons of steel. They were telling us how many thousands of tablets of an antidote were available to combat the dangers of anthrax. They were sharing with us how quickly a million people might be infected with smallpox and then how many months or years it would take before the country might be equipped with enough doses of a vaccine that has fallen into disuse.

We only pretended to be concerned about the boys and their broken hearts. Broken hearts on both sides we knew would mend. We were concerned about boys and girls together in cars and alcohol and the dangerous situations they might create and encounter. And even though they weren't old enough for us to begin that kind of worrying, we felt a kind of nostalgia for times when that was all we thought we would have to worry about, and those times were only a week old.

It was an old style ice cream parlor that sold special fancy chocolates and had booths where you could sit and eat a BLT with the soup of the day. The paintings on the wall were from a different era. There were many flavors to choose from, and the girls debated back and forth their different merits. In the end, Miabelle settled upon cookie dough and Isabel chose black raspberry. They both left holding enormous ice cream cones.

We walked down the sidewalk back towards the car. They held the ice cream cones in opposite hands, and with the other hand they held hands as they walked. They were quite a sight. No adult could pass them without commenting, or at least smiling.

Then my daughter asked me the question: "Daddy, how many licks are there in an ice cream cone?"

I said I was sure I didn't know.

So they set about like two scientists to answer the question. They began to count their licks.

At forty-two licks, I began to consider the effectiveness of ice cream as a weapon.

"Sixty-five, sixty-six, sixty-seven …" Was anything as disarming?

"Eighty-nine, ninety, ninety-one …" Sweet surrender.

Impossible as it may sound, the two genius scientists, focused and oblivious as geniuses are, came up with the identical, scientifically accurate number.

Count this among the things that count: "Daddy, there are 168 licks in an ice cream cone."

Bunny Bear

Rarely does a baby arrive alone. A new child introduces presences into your house. The father you never knew you had, disarmed by the likenesses he sees in these little eyes. The helpful mother-in-law bringing wisdom and techniques with her small suitcase. The sibling alternating between exuberance and despair, as he comes to terms with the very notion that the entire world is not a dream of his own creation, that others will take their place on the stage and act their parts.

But these noisy presences are not the ones I mean. I call your attention to those who spring fully-formed out of nowhere, the silent, watchful ones—the stuffed animals.

Like our son before her, our middle daughter was greeted on earth by an abundance of teddy bears. They came in all sizes, and in some cases, unexpected colors. I remember a pink teddy bear and a blue one. One day we lined them all up on a large sofa, and sat her among them. In my memory, we took this photograph, but I have never been able to find it, so it remains right there, vividly, in my mind, where I can call it up at will.

Because the first eighteen stuffed animals that entered my daughter's life were bears, she also called the nineteenth one "bear," despite the long, floppy ears and other features that would have made you or I identify him as "rabbit."

They were about the same size when he arrived. He had a whiteness he would never again achieve, despite endless washings. The insides of his ears were pink. He had two black button eyes.

They were inseparable from the start. She called him "bear." We called him "bunny." She continued to call him "bear." Dutifully, we corrected her by calling him "bunny." Then, one day, in a compromise of her own creation, she announced "Bunny Bear," as if he had never before been introduced to us.

He was squeezed into the high-chair with her. We were at the breakfast table.

"What is Bunny Bear going to eat today?" I joked.

She didn't respond by pointing out that he was an inanimate object in no need of sustenance.

She simply said, "He doesn't even have a mouth."

I looked and saw how right she was. Bunny Bear had eyes, and a nose, and incomparable ears, but he had no mouth. Something I had never noticed before.

One day he just disappeared. She was four or five at the time, in the habit of taking him everywhere she went. He had survived a lot, including the loss, at different times, of both ears, which had been sewn back. For years, he had been weathered gray.

Now, he was missing. She was inconsolable. The house had been turned upside down. The car had been ransacked. We burst open the doors to rooms without search warrants. But no sign of Bunny Bear.

Word got out. Concerned relatives and friends called. E-mails flew. Everyone checked their houses, as if he could have snuck in when they weren't looking. Even the neighbor with the voice of gravel, who hardly ever spoke, said to me while he picked up his newspaper, "I hear you lost Bunny Bear."

Now that we had lost him, we realized how many lives he had entered.

I sat down with my daughter and we did something we have done many times since.

"When you can't find something," I said. "You have to stop looking everywhere, and find it in your mind."

Together, we went over the last three days. It included a car ride. There had been a rest stop with a children's play area. In all of our thinking, Bunny Bear had been with us the next day, but she couldn't tell me anywhere she had been with him after that visit to the rest stop.

I went out to the car by myself. Everyone was getting ready for bed. I drove fifteen or twenty miles down the parkway, wondering what the chances were that some other child in some other state wasn't clutching Bunny Bear right now. How would she even know his name?

It took quite a bit of persuasion to get the security guard to open the play area. He swore to me that there was no stuffed animal of that description in the lost and found, and that the place was emptied of such items daily.

I found him, though. He was lying on his side on the metal windowsill, with kids' books and magazines on either side of him, as if he had just been shoved there, as if no one would ever look at him again.

The expression on the guard's face said, "That's what all this fuss is about?" No doubt he was childless.

I sat Bunny Bear in the front seat. I buckled his seat belt.

For the entire ride home, he was his quiet self. I didn't say a word either, but I kept looking over at him and thinking about how thoroughly beauty and meaning, and even individuality, depend upon the investments we make.

Phone Call

My father, now in his late seventies, fell and broke his hip. He reached up to pick a peach from one of the trees he and my mother had planted years ago, but the branch, as if reluctant to give up its fruit, would not let go. The pull that finally got him the peach also sent him to the ground, prize in hand.

You need to know that my parents are hardy people used to doing things their own way, without anyone else's help. You also need to know that even though my father is an educated man with a scientific background, he does not trust doctors. The last place he would ever want to find himself is in a hospital. And the third thing you need to know is that breaking a hip has tremendous emotional meaning for my father. His mother broke her hip in her eighties and was never the same again. Against his protests, she was soon put in a nursing home by his brother and sisters, where she died at the age of 92. We have all spent considerable time over the years assuring him that he will never see the inside of a nursing home.

So it is with this sequence of imagined events in mind—ambulance, hospital, nursing home—that my father persuaded my mother, even though he could not move, that he was not really hurt, that all he needed was to get back to the comfort and safety of the house, some one hundred yards away, and that everything else would take care of itself.

It is nearly ten years now that my parents have lived on what we call "the farm"—a 2 ½-acre stretch of land they truly love. They've planted it with every fruit and vegetable that you can imagine, and bright, beautiful flowers make it the marvel of visitors and passersby. The prestigious garden section of the NY Times found fit to write an article about it.

The first time family and friends were invited to the farm, more showed up than expected. As the planned outdoor lunch drew near, my mother realized that she didn't have a table large enough to seat everyone.

"Dad," she said, "you'd better build a table." And he did. Within twenty minutes, he had cut the planks of wood with his power saw, and nailed them together. Soon, everyone was talking loudly and eating stuffed shells and ziti.

In the same spirit, my mother, half the size of my father, somehow managed to get him off the ground and over to the house. She did it with the help of a wheelbarrow. While I was not there to see it, I don't believe the image will ever leave me.

The doctors confirmed that he had broken his hip. He began a hospital stay of several weeks during which they successfully placed a pin into his body. I called him every few days to see how he was doing. He was not a pleasant patient. For the first time in his life he admitted to me that he was in pain, and that he planned to ask the hospital staff for stronger painkillers. This kind of thinking had always been anathema to him.

One day, I dialed the number to his room.

"Dad."

"Yeah."

"How are you?"

"Okay."

"How's the pain?"

"Oh, it's okay," he said slowly.

"Are they giving you painkillers?"

"Yeah, they are." His words were slurred, and tailing off.

"Your voice sounds different."

"Well, they're giving me a lot of these painkillers."

"Are you alright?"

"I'm so glad you called me," he said, uncharacteristically. "Your mother said you wouldn't call, but I said you would. I knew you would," he insisted.

Then I realized, all of a sudden, that I was not talking to my father. They must have moved him to physical therapy, as they had been promising to do, any day.

"They're going to take me now," he said, as brightly as he could muster. "Wish me luck."

I did not have the heart to disappoint him, so I embraced the deception. I wished him luck.

Poets House

My 14-year old son signed up for five classes at the Scratch DJ Academy in New York City. The advertising for the course had promised that with the right dedication and a good ear, you could become a Ph. DJ in no time.

He had his own set of turntables. Walking up the stairs at night, I could sometimes hear the smooth scratching sounds coming from his room. Now he had signed up for the class, and I had volunteered to drive him.

He had been born in the city. At the age of four, we moved him with his one-year old sister to the suburbs. As we were driving to his first class, he announced that he wished he lived in the city. It was a rare offering these days—an unsolicited opinion.

I decided to agree.

"I know what you mean," I said. I missed the city myself, especially now with its wounded bustle. We were heading to Soho, a familiar mix of street vendors, galleries, tourists, village people, students, junkies, and rising DJ's.

No sooner had we entered the car, than he popped one of his CD's into the player. This time I was determined to hear the words. I asked him about the story in the song. He told me that the song was about a time in the future. From cut to cut, the story continued. I heard the scratching in the background and asked whether different records produced different scratching sounds.

"Definitely," he answered.

I thought about music as a weapon of expression between the generations. My parents had thought that the Dylan songs I listened to hundreds, no thousands of times, sounded foreign and ridiculous. "It's not singing," my father said.

Certainly, rock and roll had been the supreme musical revolt of a generation. I remember the teenagers in my town, shirts out and hair slicked back rocking and rolling through the fifties, prelude to their tours of duty in faraway Vietnam.

"It's not so different, your music," I said. "It has rhymes like some poetry, and sometimes it tells a story."

Lower Broadway was a stream of humanity. It was also a stream of cars, and of course there was nowhere to park. We were right up against the starting time for the class, so reluctantly I let him go from the car into the dark building, and said I would soon follow to make sure he had arrived. He wanted none of that, but I insisted, and he relented. "I'll see you shortly," I said. A few minutes after he disappeared, I called the Scratch DJ Academy to make sure that he had made it up to the sixth floor.

In front of the building, a hawker was urging passersby to go to the third floor where a massive clothing sale was underway. "Ladies," he kept repeating, "there are six thousand pairs of shoes waiting for you on the third floor." It created a frightening image—a bloody stampede of disembodied shoes.

The elevator was out of order. It meant I had to walk up six flights in the August heat. At the top, I found a series of dark rooms. In several of them, groups of kids, all wearing baseball hats backwards, were practicing their art—making music out of scratches, scratching their way to music.

I never think of myself as older than anyone else. Clearly, I was not one of them, but I would have had to see myself standing there in front of a mirror to fully grasp that. Looking out, I looked with the same eyes I had always had and if I looked older than everyone else here, I didn't see older. Age was not something I thought about very much.

I saw my son, but I knew better than to let him see that I saw him. Everyone seemed nice enough and fully absorbed in what they were doing. An attractive girl dressed in the same pronounced but casual fashion as the boys in the room told me the class would run for an hour and a half. So I left, checking my watch, and planning my descent down six flights.

Once on the street, I walked towards my own destination. I passed a wall of street vendors selling paintings, selling African figure art, including a chess set I liked, selling incense and smoking paraphernalia, selling belts and other leather goods, selling pocketbooks made from unexpected materials, selling screen plays for every movie and television show you could imagine, selling books, selling video-tapes and CD's, selling sketches made of you right on the spot.

At the end of this outdoor mall of sorts, I found myself on Spring Street. I passed a few galleries and stood in front of Poets House. A sign on the door announced that if it was past 1PM to press the buzzer and someone would come down. I pressed and a young woman came down. We went back up in the elevator together.

Poets House is a reading room lined with books. It was the invention of Stanley Kunitz, a poet now in his nineties, once our poet laureate. All of the books in Poets House have been donated—more than 30,000. They range from the best known volumes to the most obscure pamphlets. They comprise the single largest concentration of poetry in the country.

My mission was to research the poetry of the Japanese haiku master, Issa. Until recently, I had not considered the haiku form worthy of attention. To me, it had just meant an exceedingly short poem. But then I took to studying the form. I now recognized its elegance, how the syllable counts worked, how it achieved its effect by the juxtaposition of two unlike elements to create a single image.

From a difficult, painful life, Issa produced thousands of examples of spare, beautiful verse:

> The autumn evening
> It is far from a light thing
> To be born a man

On our way home:

> Rapping in the car
> The poetry of oneness
> We scratch the surface

A Death in the Family

My wife thought it would be best if I delivered the news to our eleven-year old daughter.

I asked both girls to sit down in the living room, the eleven-year old and the seven-year old.

Before I could say anything, the older one announced: "I know."

"What?"

"Petunia died. I felt her. She's all stiff."

"Oh no," said the younger one, with tears in her voice. "Your hamster died?"

"She's all stiff," the older one repeated. "And her eyes are open."

"People die with their eyes open," the younger one reported. "Unless they die when they're sleeping."

We found a round, see-through tupperware coffin for Petunia. My daughter lined it with a paper towel.

"We should make holes in it for air," the younger one said.

"We don't need to," the older one said. She wrote a brief eulogy with a magic marker on an unlined index card. "Good-bye to Petunia. She was a great friend to me. May she have fun in hamster heaven. I love you." We put the card in the coffin so the words showed through.

She asked me to bury Petunia in the backyard, behind the swing.

"Is it okay if I'm not there?" she said.

"Sure, I'll do it."

"I want to be there," the younger one said.

I went into the garage for the spade. It was a rainy, fall morning. The ground was covered with leaves. As I began to dig the hole, the cat and the dog arrived, and took sitting positions at a respectful distance. They seemed overly curious and quiet, suffering, no doubt, from survivor's syndrome.

I dug the hole, round and deep. I didn't want the dog's curiosity to turn him into a grave robber at some later date.

As the hole deepened, I thought of my grandfather, as I always did at burials of any kind. He had come to this country from Sicily in 1910. He had never learned to read, but in nearly every picture we have of him, he is holding a newspaper; his cover-up. Somehow, he managed to raise ten children through the depression on the salary of a ditch-digger.

As soon as the dirt begins to hit the coffin, I think about how having lived his life digging ditches, he refused to be buried underground. He rests in a mausoleum with my grandmother. I always wonder what he knew or saw that made him reach this conclusion.

Then I think about how my thinking about him is the only kind of earthly proof we have of living on—in the memories of those who knew us.

At the end of this brief ceremony, I thought we should go for a life-affirming walk. My daughter was all for it, and so was the dog, who makes me pause whenever I feel like he's reading my mind. He immediately began running up and down the driveway, pointing the way, making us feel like yeah, you can do it, come on, it's easy. This way!

"You can't go in your pajamas," I said to my daughter. "You have to put clothes on."

"Mommy lets me ride my bike in my pajamas."

"You have to put clothes on if you want to come with me. At least put on pants." She disappeared into the house.

My wife arrived back from an errand.

"Did you do it?" she wanted to know.

"Yeah."

"Where?"

"In the backyard, behind the swing."

"Oh, God," she said. "I hope you didn't cut the wire for the dog's invisible fence." She ran to the check the monitoring device on the porch.

Luckily, I hadn't cut the wire. My daughter came out wearing a different pair of pajama pants and holding a child-sized Mickey Mouse umbrella.

"I said put on pants."

"I changed my pants."

"I meant real pants, not another pair of pajama pants."

"These are thicker, Daddy. They're warm."

"What about socks?" The tops of her bare feet were showing in her clogs.

"I don't need socks."

"You do need socks. It's cold."

"No, it isn't."

"Get the socks or you're not going."

I took the umbrella from her and with exaggerated, reluctant gestures, she went back into the house.

Meanwhile the scout dog intensified his activities, pointing the simple way off the property again and again with increasing fervor. I put him on the leash, which he recognized as an official commitment to the walk. That calmed him down.

My daughter came back wearing socks.

"Okay," I said.

"Wait," she said. "I need gloves."

"You don't need gloves," I said.

"Yes, I do, Daddy. It's cold."

"Not cold enough for gloves."

"Yes, it's cold. I need gloves," and she ran back into the house. I knew this meant she would have to go up to the attic, where the out-of-season clothes were kept and rummage through all of the cedar chests until she found a pair of gloves that fit her hands and matched her outfit. It could take hours.

I stood there waiting under the Mickey Mouse umbrella, holding the dog at the end of the leash in my other hand.

Despite the untimely passage of Petunia, life continued on its herky-jerky, unalterable course.

The Walk

The great oak that towers above our house drops its acorns every other year. This is one of those years.

The tree is more than a hundred feet tall. Whenever strong winds accompany rain, you will see branches strewn throughout our town in the aftermath. Sometimes entire trees come crashing to the ground. The mayor, who also works another job, explained to me that each of these storms costs the town significant dollars, especially when falling branches take electric lines down with them.

In an exceptionally sad occurrence, a tree fell on a car, killing a baby.

I was standing at the end of the long driveway with the dog, holding the Mickey Mouse umbrella, waiting for my seven-year old to reappear for our walk. The hamster had died this morning, and we had buried her in the backyard. Now we were taking a restorative life-affirming walk in her memory.

Despite all of my efforts to keep the path clear, the driveway was cluttered with acorns. They were falling fiercely right now in the morning wind, banging against the roof, the drainpipe, and the ground in a cacophony of sounds. The cars were parked in the street, out of harm's way. A few days ago, I had watched the postman glide down the driveway falteringly as if he were on ice skates, then right himself at the last moment. Our neighbor with the one-year old never visited anymore unless the child had a baby bicycle helmet snugly in place.

My daughter finally appeared like a model in an outfit entirely of her own choosing: pajama tops and bottoms from two different sets, a short jacket, rainbow socks, clogs, and over-sized mittens. I met her with the umbrella as she came down the runway to protect her from the threat overhead.

Once we were off the property, the dog discovered the world all over again; the trees, the grass, the leaves. We walked on a multi-colored carpet of leaves. We could barely see the sidewalk. The news had reported that the fallen foliage was especially heavy this year, due to weather patterns. Even the commuter lines had been affected; the trainmen were having difficulty keeping the tracks clear.

We made our way down the familiar block and turned at the corner. We were still several weeks from Thanksgiving, but one of the houses was already decked out in Christmas lights. It prompted a question: "Daddy, is there really a Santa Claus?"

"What makes you ask that?" I was holding one of her mittened hands, and guiding the dog's leash with my other hand.

"How would he get into a house like that one?"

The house she was pointing at had no chimney, only a tiny metal protrusion at the top that looked like a periscope.

"Santa can also come in through the door."

"How, if it's locked?"

It reminded me of the night when her older brother, younger than she was now at the time, lay in his bed staring at the ceiling. He had lost his first tooth during the day. It was safely tucked under his pillow in anticipation of a reward.

"Is something wrong?" I asked him.

In his characteristic way of getting right to the point, he asked: "How's that fairy getting in?" On another occasion, his grandmother had asked him how he had come upon such a beautiful Easter basket. He responded with, "Some rabbit gave it to me."

"You don't remember the super in the building where we lived in the city before you were born. He had a key to get in everywhere, and sometimes he could even get in when he didn't have a key. It's like that with Santa."

"What about the alarm and the police?"

"The police understand that it's Christmas."

"Well, then if was a robber, I would rob a house on Christmas."

I decided that she might be getting too bright for her own good, and that going forward I had better concentrate on keeping her on the right side of the law. The rain picked up and the leaves were falling all around.

"Daddy?"

"Yes."

"Does God know Santa Claus?"

"I suppose He does since Santa Claus' real name is Saint Nicholas and God must know all the saints."

"Do they drink egg nog together?"

"At Christmastime, sure," I said.

"I like egg nog," she announced.

"Me too."

We had made it all the way around the block and back to the house. The oak tree didn't seem to have many more leaves to drop. As to the acorns, who knew, they were too high up to see. Soon there would be a snowman on the front lawn to greet us.

Uncle-hood

To become an uncle and to become a father are very different passages, especially if you become an uncle first. If you become a father first, there's hardly enough room for the complete uncle experience. Parenthood in the early years tends to crowd out all other relationships.

Unlike fatherhood, uncle-hood is always involuntary, like being born. It may be the only change in status a man can achieve without taking any action, or making even a single decision. There are surprising benefits, too. Women seem to find few pictures as attractive as that of a young man and a young child for whom he obviously cares. When it turns out that the man is not a father after all, well …

If the uncle is unmarried, he has more to learn about life and himself from his new role. The married uncle, even if childless, is already grounded, already on a designated path. The unmarried uncle is in a better position to approach this new experience as a sampling of possible things to come, including marriage. He is like a prospective customer at the ice cream stand, invited with tiny spoons to taste as many flavors as he wishes, but with no commitment to buy.

Being an uncle is a part-time job. When the day ends, the unmarried uncle can return to the comfortable disarray of his bachelor existence feeling like a better man, but with no fewer options than he had the day before. He can call in otherwise engaged at any time and no one can complain. Uncles are only auditing the class; as a father, you take an exam every day.

I became an uncle on the first day of summer. Ahead of me, I had five years of unmarried uncle-hood. I mention the season because it matters. Baby that he was, my first nephew spent his first fall and winter indoors. One December afternoon, eighteen months after his birth, I stood with him on the front lawn of my sister's house and experienced my first uncle epiphany. Snow had suddenly begun to fall all around us—big, wet flakes. He held both hands out and looked skyward. For more than a year he had lived on the earth crawling and walking through its fullness, but never had he encountered anything like this. The very idea that the flakes were melting as soon as they hit his hands, yet accumulating all around us on the ground, put a look on his face that produced my epiphany. It was this: that through the eyes of a child we discover the world all over again.

I had many similar moments, but the next memorable one took place in the opposite season—summer—on the beach. I was a married-without-children uncle now, and we had taken my nephew to the beach for the day. We bought him a kite on a perfect kite day—sunny and windy. I showed him how by running along the beach he could make the wind catch the kite and lift it. With the kite hundreds of feet on the air, I showed him how to keep it steady and control its movement by tugging lightly at the stick wrapped with cord. He was a little man standing shirtless on the beach, captain of an aircraft sailing through the sky. My second epiphany was this: that by teaching a child how to do something we learn how to do it all over again.

On the day I became a father, the nephew who made me an uncle was eight years old. The hospital had a rule that only the baby's brothers and sisters would be allowed in to see him. Because the children were so excited to see their new cousin, the grownups told them to pretend to be his brothers and sisters. They all did, except my oldest nephew.

Because he did not want to pretend, and because he did not want to displease others, and because he had an infinite soul even at a very young age, he sat down in the hospital lobby instead with a piece of paper and his only writing implement—a green crayon. He made a drawing of a green sun rising over the green horizon, and spelled out in simple, big letters: "WELCOME TO THE WORLD. HOPE YOU LIKE IT." My fifteen-year old son still has this greeting framed on his mantelpiece.

Myrtle Tree

If you've done something foolish, and you're afraid that people will find out, there's an easy way to take care of that worry. Tell everyone.

We were driving through Virginia, on our way to a vacation in the Outer Banks when I first saw the trees. They resembled bright bouquets of flowers—always either purple or magenta—and they were everywhere. Compared to its background, each tree stood out like an exceptionally beautiful woman in a group of nondescript friends.

Amazed as I was by the tree itself, I was even more surprised to find out its name. "Myrtle," to me, was a somewhat dated name for an older woman. It was also the name of a long avenue in Brooklyn, New York, which I had always assumed had been named for just such an older woman.

I decided that I needed a picture of at least one of these trees. However, as often happens when a picture presents itself, I didn't have a camera. Besides, we were part of a caravan of four cars hurrying to a carefully planned, long desired vacation, and stopping everything even for the time it takes for a snapshot would have been out of the question. I contented myself with the thought that once we reached our destination, there would be plenty of time to photograph myrtle.

The week ahead will always be memorable—for the beach, the sunsets and the sunrises, the wild horses, the restaurants, the houses, and best of all, the company—old friends in a new setting—but the myrtle tree did not grow so far south. I would have to wait for the trip home to take the picture.

After such a great week, the drive north was a little like letting the air out of a balloon. The first day back would also be the first day of school, so all of the mothers were intent upon a speedy return, and all of the kids were in a bad mood.

Soon, the myrtle trees appeared once again, in all their splendor, but there was no stopping the caravan. A sequence of cell phone calls from car to car established a breakfast place ahead where we would all meet.

A mile before the rendezvous point, I saw a myrtle tree attractively placed in front of some railroad tracks. I finished my breakfast hurriedly, and made my way out of the restaurant, promising to be right back. I had borrowed a digital camera from one of the other fathers, confiding my plan to him.

I was there in minutes. I parked the car alongside the road and quickly snapped the photograph. I got back in the car, mindful of the breakfast, and headed back towards the restaurant. Had I simply continued, everything would have been fine, but I saw another tree along the tracks, fuller, brighter, more beautiful, and I decided that I needed just one more photograph.

I parked the car and exited more hurriedly now. Cars were whizzing by in the background as I framed the picture and snapped.

When I turned back to the car, the rapid part of the nightmare began. It lasted as long as it took me to try all four doors in succession and find them all locked, as long as it took me to spy the keys dangling from the ignition and the second set of keys lying uselessly in the dashboard tray.

The long part of the nightmare included a mile walk back to the restaurant, stopping along the way at two service stations, the apologies, the two-hour wait while the helpful service man arrived and worked the door open with his special tools, and the incredibly long silence during the impossibly long trip home. Despite my pleas to continue home without us, the other three families had waited it out.

I tried to joke that I had extended a great vacation by two hours, but no one smiled. In the end, I only had this to offer:

> Myrtle, Myrtle …
>
> I had no idea
> that you
> could be like this,

that you would put
such color
in the world.

Now that I
have stepped
outside myself

and come
to see you
as you are,

please don't let
the door be locked.

Toast

As I raised the champagne glass, a memory elbowed its way to the front of my prepared speech.

When my brother was only three years old, I was in my ninth year. Our oldest sister was six. Our younger sister would not be in her crib for another full year.

One day our mother asked my sister and me to walk to the grocery store to pick up some things. That was a few decades ago, when people in America still walked places, and even more astonishingly, children moved about unaccompanied.

If there was any worry, it all had to do with the two side streets we would have to cross. She made us promise to hold hands and look both ways.

We asked if we could bring our little brother.

She paused for a thoughtful moment, and then said okay, but she made us double and triple promise to be careful crossing the streets, especially now that we would have the baby with us.

We left feeling as if we were on a grownup mission, intensely focused on the list of items, which I held, and mindful of the two crossings we would have to make to reach our destination.

The houses in the town where we grew up are simple brick structures. Occasionally, we passed a wooden house painted gray or white. In my memory it is a warm spring day. There are new leaves on the trees, and sometimes a bird flutters by.

I can still see the first street. Carefully and deliberately we looked both ways, and then carefully we crossed.

When we reached the second street, once again, we looked both ways, and once again we crossed very carefully.

We turned right at the avenue. The grocery store was located in the middle of the block. As you entered, you saw three checkout counters. Off to the side, a pyramid of peach cans was under construction. Only the three broadest, bottom layers had been built. We brought our little brother over to the pyramid, which reached the height of his chest, and asked him to wait there until we came back.

My sister and I had the serious business of the list to handle.

Down the aisles we moved, like a married couple in a miniature land, reaching for products, checking brands, sizes, and prices. We counted the items on the list and the items in the basket a dozen times. Satisfied that we had completed the job, we moved to the check out and headed home.

The trip back always seems shorter than the trip there.

We crossed the first street with caution and care. We crossed the second street even more carefully, knowing it was our last marker.

I put the bag of groceries down on the kitchen table. Together we presented the list, convinced that nothing had been forgotten.

But we were mistaken, and Mom picked up on it right away.

"Where is your brother?" she said.

Our ability to react in the frantic minutes that followed is a sign of those times. Like most families, we had a car, but like most families we only had one car, and it was what Dad used to get to work.

I got on the next speediest means of transportation in the house, my bicycle, and raced down the three blocks back to the store, paying attention at the crossings, but certainly not like we had before.

I burst into the store and found my brother in the same position we had left him, with his head resting in his hand and his elbow bent on the peach cans. He hadn't even realized we left the store. He stood there patiently as he did now, next to his new bride, waiting for me to begin this toast.

Hospital

Hospitals exhibit a special kind of sensory depravation. The walls are always painted pale colors that call no attention to themselves—off-white, cream, weak green, and the lightest yellow. The floors all seem to have come from the same linoleum supplier. They all reflect fluorescent light back up towards the ceiling in the same way.

I'm sure there are good reasons for this. Maybe the benefactors of hospital wings would be upset if they felt that their contributions were going towards lavish furnishings. Maybe colorful surroundings would be just too excitable for certain medical conditions. Or maybe it's just that the human dramas taking place within these walls are so full of the excruciating colors of real life that best keep the walls themselves as close as possible to blank canvases.

We brought our 14-year old son to the hospital on the scheduled day. The surgery would be minor, but there was general anesthesia involved, and however high the rate of success and however infinitesimal the chances that something would go awry, we harbored the anxiety only a parent can know, whatever age the child.

Putting on the yellow paper gowns so that we could enter the recovery room, I could not help but travel back to the first time I had worn one of these—the day, or night, I should say—of his birth.

In the 26th hour of my wife's labor, the decision was made to go for a c-section. Back then, husbands were not allowed into the operating room for caesarians. After weeks of Lamaz classes, I found myself pacing back and forth in the waiting room.

It was late. I was alone in the room, which existed at the end of a long corridor. It was the next to last day of February in a leap year, and it was after 11PM. We had been through several shifts of nurses. A new head nurse with a pronounced Irish accent had just assured me that as soon as there was news to tell she would deliver it personally. I continued to pace.

Suddenly, the nurse appeared in the long corridor. She walked towards me and I prepared myself to find out that everything had gone incredibly well, I could only hope, and whether we would be holding hands with a little girl or a little boy for years to come. But no, after about twenty steps she turned left into one of the adjoining rooms.

I began to pace again. As the clock ticked towards the midnight hour, part of me felt that it would be unique and interesting to have a baby with a leap year birthday. Another part of me thought it might be difficult for the child.

Once again, the nurse walked down the long corridor towards me. She passed the open room on her left and once again I prepared myself for the big news, and, once again, she disappeared before reaching me, this time to the right. I stood there with my hands on the sides of my head. The night through the windows was astonishingly dark. It sounded like a light rain had picked up.

Now I found myself pacing harder, this time with my hands in my pockets. I counted the change in each pocket by feel, over and over, separating the subway tokens from the coins. I tried to sit down with my hands folded in my lap; I lasted less than a minute. None of the magazines on the table captured my attention; they were dog-eared. By contrast, the newspaper looked as if it had just been printed, but I knew it didn't have the news I wanted.

When I looked up, she was coming down the corridor again. She passed the exit to the left. She passed the exit to the right. She continued to walk towards me. When she was ten yards away, she said: "It's a boy. 11-16."

I thought for a moment and said, "Why isn't it twelve?" without considering how big a baby this would be.

"That's not the weight," she said. "It's the time."

Now, here we were, fourteen years later, almost to the day, and the patient was doing fine this time, too.

Godfather

When I was nineteen years old, I took a trip that would be difficult to duplicate today. I purchased a roundtrip ticket for a flight that would land in London and return from Paris 85 days later. I went alone, because my high school friend chickened out at the last minute. I had just finished my freshman year in college, I had never been on an airplane, and I had never been more than a hundred miles from my home.

I visited these countries: England, Belgium, France, Holland, Italy, Greece, Turkey, and Morocco. I hitchhiked everywhere and stayed in youth hostels. I had more adventures than I could ever recount, but the one I am thinking about today has to do with the visit I made to my father's godfather.

His first name was Vitale. I visited him about the 70th day of my trip, now a seasoned traveler. I had taken a boat from Naples to Palermo, and followed the directions of people in the street until I found his house. He had no idea I was coming. As I neared the house, more and more people told me that they knew the man I was seeking. The last guide brought me right to the door and explained who I was before I said anything.

Of course, Vitale remembered his godson. He introduced me to his wife, whom he said had not left Palermo for twenty years, but as it happened, she was on her way today to visit her mother in the country, who was about to celebrate her 100th birthday.

I was struck by how cool the house was despite the intense heat outside. There was no sign of air-conditioning. Vitale explained that the building materials produced the coolness.

"Sicily is an old country," he announced to me. "We learned long ago what we need to know."

He spoke completely intelligible English with a heavy accent.

His story was different from that of the other immigrants to America. He had stayed for twenty years, splitting his time between Brooklyn and New Orleans, and then returned. There is a faded photograph of my father as a boy, seated with his godfather in a car with an open top.

He was what the Italians in Brooklyn called "educato," I can remember my father telling me, though in what, or about what, was never clear.

My grandparents, by contrast, had each said good-bye to their own parents at the age of 19 or 20, never to set foot again in the land of their birth. It occurred to me that I was the first in a family of more than a hundred offspring to stand on this soil.

Vitale took me for a walk through the town. He had very little hair left, wore a canvas hat, and carried a cane. He brought me to a cafe where we drank small cups of very strong espresso. He suggested I try a certain pastry, with an unforgettable taste that I can summon up today in my mind, but which I have never been able to find again, and whose name, regrettably, I do not know.

Sitting across from him back in his living room at a large mahogany table later that day, I watched him elaborately cut a pear into bite-size pieces.

I was interested in his experience, in his choice to repatriate. This trip was more than an adventure for me. It was an exploration. I was considering living in Europe.

"Do you miss anything about America?" I asked.

"Oh yes," he said, and paused, while I waited to hear something about liberty, freedom of expression, an ever-expanding horizon of possibilities.

"Shredded Wheat," he said. "I can't find it anywhere."

Barefoot Girl

There have been many times when I did not say anything. Many times I could not think of anything to say. People sometimes conclude that the person not speaking has something he will not divulge.

In deep summer, there is a quiet road greener than any other road I have ever seen. There is a low, stone wall built by hand, and an impressive house set far behind the wall.

In that house, your parents had lived. I met them on separate occasions. As you explained, "My mother cannot bear to see my father anymore."

There was a piano in the room. Your mother played the piano. She played lively tunes through the afternoon, then retired to her room. She was a decent enough woman with a pleasant disposition, but she seemed overwhelmed by life. In the middle of the day, she often had to lie down, you told me.

On the mantelpiece were the pictures of your sister and brother, as young children. Your sister wanted no part of the family anymore. Your brother had been cut down at the age of nine by a racing automobile, in front of the family house.

Your father was tall, and handsome. When I first saw him, he was standing against the wall in your living room, the room with the piano. You took him by the hand, and we went to the kitchen where we sat all three at the table.

He told me he had once opened an agency in Darien. Then he looked at you with loving eyes, and said, "Barefoot girl with cheek of tan."

He turned back to me and repeated that he had once opened an agency in Darien, but things had not worked out. "No, not at all," he said. Things hadn't worked out.

He looked at you again, and again he said: "Barefoot girl with cheek of tan."

We left the splendor of your house and the greenness of your yard behind to drive to a restaurant. Your father, a young man, not yet fifty years old, sat in the back of the car. He leaned forward and told me that he had once opened an agency in Darien, but things had not worked out.

We went to a Friendly's or a Howard Johnson's, I don't remember which. We waited for a table where a party of six was finishing up. Between the time the diners stood up and the waiter arrived to clear up the table, your father sat in one of the chairs. Quickly, he began to drink all of the partially finished sodas.

"No, Dad," you said. "No, don't do that. Don't do that." You sat down next to him and took his hand.

He looked into your eyes as if he knew he was in a predicament. Then he called you "his barefoot girl with cheek of tan."

He turned to me as if we had just met, and told me he had once had an agency in Darien, but things had just not worked out.

As the afternoon drew to a close, you asked me to please take your father into the backyard, and to talk to him, because you had to bring him back to the institution, and that he would not want to go, that he would get very upset and try to get back into the house, and to please not let him do it, while you locked all the doors.

He was taller than I was. I began to talk to him about the agency in Darien, but he knew right away what was going on. I covered him as I would have in a game of half-court basketball, trying to impede his progress without making any physical contact. I watched his eyes, as I would have on the court.

They grew desperate. He broke away and ran downfield for a long pass, in the final seconds of the game. His team was losing. He ran full tilt towards the goal post of the door. I ran alongside of him. We arrived together. He reached for the handle, only to find it already locked. He sank to his knees in despair.

We left in separate cars—you with your father and me on my way back to my city apartment.

I don't know where you are now, but I do know that I never looked into your eyes and told you how courageous I felt you were. I should have repeated it for you, over and over and over.

Anniversary

At the last moment, instead of ushering them into the usual dining room, the hostess abruptly and inexplicably guided them into the ballroom, where they were greeted in a rush by the friends of their youth, the friends of their middle age, and the children of those friends. From the look on their faces, it was that rare thing—a successful surprise party—on the eve of their fiftieth anniversary.

There was a wall of gifts, a bar in each corner of the room, an impressive buffet, a cake as wide as the table that held it, the clink of glasses, the growing crescendo of chatter that builds when people who have not seen each other for significant amounts of time try to fill the gap with talk, but there was also something more: one of the four children hosting this party was dying.

I always thought it would be interesting to graph the sound level of a cocktail party. As people arrive, the sound naturally increases. The louder it gets, the louder people speak in order to be heard so it gets louder still. Add alcohol as a factor and the loudness increases further, until people begin to leave and the sound level drops. As the sound level drops, people can speak less loudly and the sound level drops further, until everyone is gone except for the people cleaning up.

Here, though, it was different. There were great pauses in the crescendo. Even the simplest of us could not leave this gathering without understanding that rarely in life is only one drama being staged. For every current there are many undercurrents. The sound did not rise in its usual mindless way, because the party's attention was fractured, because we could not help but be mindful of the movements of the beautiful, dying woman, our friend.

It did matter that she was beautiful. Beauty always matters. It mattered to us that she was more beautiful than ever, that the endless regimens she endured had reduced her so, that she looked again like the girl of her youth while still the wife and mother of two. It mattered that her blue violet eyes were more compelling than ever, and it mattered that all of this beauty made her more attractive to us. It mattered because it added to the cruelty of the situation.

On the surface, the party moved through its pre-ordained steps. The children and the grandchildren gave small speeches made up of amusing anecdotes and other memories. Some of the cards were read, some of the gifts were opened. She stood off to the side during all of this. Involuntarily, as a group, we began to transform our feelings about her beauty into feelings about courage and the desire to live. When she became visibly upset about something, we all felt upset, in whatever part of the room we stood.

Then the music began to play, and with it a third drama began to play for my wife and me. We had been at one other event in the past month where there was music and a feeling of solemnity. Our friend, the composer, had committed suicide. At his request, in a high-ceilinged church in lower Manhattan, they played his symphony at the funeral mass, his last work, his musical suicide notes.

Now, she began to dance with her father. It was a slow dance. My wife and I joined them. I was thinking about our two young daughters. I was trying to remember that phrase from the Greek historian, Herodotus, about how war inverts the natural order: "In peace sons bury fathers, but in war fathers bury sons." When do fathers bury daughters?

As I watched them, I could see that even in this small thing, this dance with her father she was clinging to this life. I thought about our other friend. He took his life; her life is being taken from her. "Too bad," I whispered to my wife, "they can't transplant the desire to live or the life force. Then, at least, we could have saved one of them."

In the next month, we attended another funeral and another burial. My wife will never let go of her childhood friend, Ivy. As a father, I can only imagine her father's thoughts:

> *The Gift of Ivy*
>
> Here is my Ivy.
>
> I have watched her grow
> at first underfoot

then each year a little higher
upon the stone wall.

She has made my garden into a place
of beauty and grace.

Here is my Ivy.

I give her to you
because you give me no choice.

May she temper your harsh ways.
May she bring sunlight into the garden
of your days as she has into mine.

Here is my Ivy.

Though I give her,
never can I give her up.
The tendrils of her heart
with mine intertwine.

The Enchanted Florist

It seems the Enchanted Florist has become Planet Wireless.

I suppose that might mean that nowadays we need cell phones more than freshly cut flowers. The storefront, which I pass on my daily commute, had been home to the florist for at least the last eleven years.

It has been that long since we left the city for the suburbs. We arrived in the dead of winter. Leaving in the dark winter mornings and returning after dark, it seemed like I never saw anyone. My wife, who is a natural at making friends, had hundreds of them by the time the spring brought out the dogwood and the cherry trees that make the town look like a Matisse.

Buried in my work, and still commuting to the city by car every day, I remained what she called "the invisible husband."

"And this is my husband," she would announce to a new friend, as if I were the rabbit she had just managed to pull out of her hat. She would introduce me with a flourish, with the same gesture and tone you might use when pulling the drape off a hidden piece of furniture or a new car.

I ended up meeting so many people this way, mostly women holding children by the hand, that there was no way I could keep track of them all. Often on the playground, or while I was walking the dog, a woman would wave. Not knowing who she was, and feeling guilty about it, I would immediately put on my face a look of complete recognition, and eagerly wave back.

Sometimes, this woman was not waving at me at all, but at someone behind me. Seeing the look of recognition on my face, she would catch the guilty feeling from me, thinking that she should know me, and wave back even harder. These encounters produced some of the few people in the town I had met who did not already know my wife. To everyone else, I was "Jodi's husband."

If you dropped my wife by parachute into foreign terrain, she would still make lots of friends in short order among the natives, including the local warlords and their wives. She succeeds in this so well, because it is second nature for her to focus on the other person. She gives feedback before she gets it. She has the knack.

So the question I answer most often is: "Where's Jodi?" I usually count to myself the number of seconds before the question gets asked. Most people will engage in some small conversation about something—the weather, the dog, the kids—before asking the burning question. Should a third person join us during this brief conversation, the first person will make the inevitable introduction: "Do you know Jodi's husband?"

My drive to work takes twenty-two minutes on a good day. I have about a mile of winding roads that I snake through on my way to the main route. There is a stop light at the end of this mile and then a right turn which leads to the main road. If the light is red, rather than wait for it to change, I am in the habit of turning into the parking area in front of the adjacent row of stores, then exiting the parking area ahead of the light, with a clear path to the main route.

On this particular morning, there were four or five cars stopped at the red light. I bore right as usual into the parking area to avoid the light. As soon as I did this, I noticed that there was a police car stopped at the red light in the other direction, facing me. This police car immediately put on its flashing lights, although it did not move.

Seeing the flashing lights, I decided that it was about time I got my wife flowers. At the last moment, I abruptly turned towards a parking spot in the front of the last store in the row—The Enchanted Florist.

The car behind me, on its way to the main road by the same clandestine route, promptly hit me from behind. She was driving an SUV. She pulled up parallel to me and let out a string of invectives, challenging my IQ, my sanity, my driving abilities, and the legitimacy of my birth. In the middle of this barrage, she suddenly looked at me and asked: "Are you Jodi's husband?"

"Yes, I am," I said. "See that police car over there?" The lights were still flashing. "He's coming over here to give us tickets." We both shot out of the parking area and down the main road.

There was no damage to the car. Despite my re-telling of this story to my wife and others, we could not figure out who this woman was. We still don't know.

Blackout

It is now news to no one that the Northeast, parts of the Midwest and parts of Canada were struck by a sudden and massive loss of electricity. When the blackout hit, I was involved in a call with one of my company's clients. I was looking into the computer screen. In a single instant, the life was sucked out of everything. Simultaneously, the picture was swallowed by the darkness of the screen and the voice speaking to me vanished, mid-word.

I cursed the real estate agent and the building. We had been assured that electricity and phone service, the life-blood of a software company, were flawless here. We walked down the stairway with people from businesses that share our hallway, everyone looking dazed and unsteady, as if we had all been rudely awakened from the same electronic dream. The natural light of the late afternoon made us squint.

When I reached the ground floor, my focus shifted from the possible shortcomings of the building to those of the town. I saw policemen directing traffic. The signal lights overhead were not working. I was happy to find that I could use my cell phone to call my client's office and explain. I got the receptionist and began to say that the lights had gone out. She told me her office had also experienced an outage.

"That's not possible," I said. She was two states away. "Or else, it's an incredible coincidence." Then her phone went dead.

I walked to my car, less than 50 yards away, and turned on the radio to hear only static. Then, as I moved the dial, one radio station after another announced its revival thanks to backup generators. They reported the extent of the outage. I called home to make sure everything was OK. The phones at home worked.

The house was strangely quiet when I got there. No televisions blared. The trilling sound of someone receiving a response to an instant message did not sound, loudly or faintly. No one was playing a video game or watching a DVD. We suddenly had only ourselves.

My wife calculated how she could remove all dinner items from the refrigerator in one quick opening of the door. I started the gas grill in the backyard. Soon we were all seated around the table, much earlier than usual. No one had to be torn away from what they were doing. For the moment, there was nothing else doing.

As darkness gathered, we brought out the candles and decided to play a board game by their low light. Our youngest daughter picked the game of Life from the shelf nearest her reach. In this game, you start as a single person in a car. You spin the wheel and get married. You spin again and along the way you get children—one, two, three children. You move from one job to another. There is a deck of cards that randomly deals you advances and setbacks. You make investments, and if you're lucky, you retire wealthy and happy.

We went to bed early, carrying a candle, like our image of Ben Franklin still conjuring up electricity. Blowing out the candle, I asked my wife if she remembered our last blackout, minor compared to this one.

It had only affected part of the town, and it struck close to 10 in the evening, after many of the early commuters and their families were already in bed. I was helping my son study for a history exam when the lights went out. We went to the car and sat in the driveway for the next hour or so, under the interior light, going over European history from the conquests of Napoleon right up to the assassination of Archduke Ferdinand and the devastating procession of events that followed.

Being a night person, I did not realize how early so many people in our town went to sleep. That previous outage, nearly two years ago, had disabled their alarm clocks. They woke in horror the next day to discover how late for work they were. They scrambled to catch trains and buses.

A significant number of them were still rushing toward their offices instead of sitting at their desks in the South Tower as it came crashing to the ground on that gloriously clear, fateful September morning.

Cousin John

In Italian families, there are naming conventions that were still strictly observed in the 1940's. As a result, I have five cousins on the same side of the family named John. Each of these men is unique, but only one of them owed some of his uniqueness to a medical fact that was not yet known in the year of his birth: that measles during pregnancy could have serious consequences.

Cousin John died this week, at the age of fifty-eight. According to his doctors, he had the mental capacity of an eight-year old, but these are just numbers.

John was tall and thin. At 6 foot 3 inches, he towered above his parents and his older brother, none of whom reached 5 foot 6 inches. His father died at least twenty years ago. His mother, his constant companion of 58 years, seen together with him everywhere, is a woman under five feet tall.

In his youth, his brother was a left-handed pitcher with stuff good enough to win a tryout with the Brooklyn Dodgers. They liked what they saw, but they held his lack of height against him, and it went nowhere.

John was left-handed, too. Now, he lay in a black suit the length of a very long coffin, his hands crossed. He was wearing glasses, as he sometimes did in life, and he looked very peaceful.

I did not plan to speak on the morning of the funeral until it became clear that no one else was planning to do so either. I knew the priest had been briefed with the story of John's life, but how well could he do without actually having known him.

During the mass, the priest addressed us, paying special attention to my aunt whom he could see needed comforting. She had made the decision right from the start not to institutionalize her son. She had dedicated her life to him, and now in her eighties, she worried every day about his well being in a future he might have to face without her.

The priest looked at her and explained that God always gives what is needed, and that this was His way of taking care of her worry. He said that in heaven there was no such thing as a handicap, and that even if John had not been able to enjoy life as much as you or I, he said to her, he would enjoy the same eternal reward.

Despite the priest's good intentions, there was something I felt he had not gotten right. John had enjoyed life. There was certainly nothing to say that any of us enjoyed it any more.

As the mass ended, the priest gave me a sign and I walked towards the altar, and then turned to face about thirty family members and neighbors.

"As I was driving here today, I had several memories and thoughts. You may even find one of them amusing on this solemn occasion.

"I'm not sure exactly how old my son was at the time, but he was old enough to talk and he loved everything about dinosaurs. We had just returned from a family gathering at my parents' farm. I found him sitting in front of a long line of dinosaurs he had just set up. He'd named each dinosaur for a family member. Uncle Angelo was an alligator. Aunt Jean was in the line and so were my mother and father and everyone else. Johnny was the tallest dinosaur of all, and next to him was the smallest one. "Who's that?" I asked, and he said to me, "That's Johnny's little friend," by which he meant John's mother, Aunt Mary.

"Nobody ever really leaves, as long as the people he knew remember him, and Johnny was unforgettable. None of us will ever forget him.

"At different times in our lives we learn different things—things like how to get into school, how to get out of school, how to compete in the world, how to be a parent—but it seems to me that the most important thing to learn is how to recognize the gifts being given to you each day. And Johnny gave us so many gifts.

"First, he made us understand in a very deep way that it's acceptable to be different, that you could still be worthy of love and capable of great love.

"I remember a day when I was very young and I went on a long walk with him through a bewildering patchwork of Brooklyn streets in his old neighborhood. We were doing errands, or maybe I was the errand, being dropped off somewhere. Johnny knew exactly where he was going at all times. He never wavered at any corner, and along the way everyone greeted him. He knew all of their names.

Johnny always knew everybody's name—a talent people in important places would pay a lot to have.

"And he knew everyone's voice, too. All he needed was a few syllables over the phone and he always knew who was calling.

"Maybe Johnny's biggest gift to us is this: He reminds us that innocence can exist in the world, something we need to remember more than ever these days.

"So Aunt Mary, Aunt Jean, everyone … don't worry about Johnny. On this next leg of the journey, Johnny knows the way."

We left the church for our vehicles. In a long procession, the cars left the parking lot for the cemetery, headlights turned on to signal to the rest of the traffic our separateness and purpose. My car was last. After the burial, I would have a two-hour drive back to my office where I knew the work was piling up. We moved from the local streets to the expressway and then off the expressway to the highway and then back to local streets again and then onto another highway. A car got between my car and the next car in the procession, and then another. I was forced to stop at a red light. My attention lapsed. I lost the group. Even though I had been on these streets before, and visited this exact cemetery, today I could not find it, and never did. I lacked John's sense of direction.

Rivalry

I was astonished to learn that the 2004 baseball season would be the twenty-fifth since Bucky Dent's famous home-run. On the day of that event, I had just completed a nine-month assignment to write a dictionary for IBM. I had just spent the last night in my rented upstate house. I had just sold my car because I knew I would no longer need it back in my true home, New York City. I stopped for a moment in a local bar in Woodstock to check out the score of the game. I ended up staying for all nine innings.

A small, black and white television hung above the bar. The place was filled with the usual Woodstock populace, mostly long-haired, bearded men. I had lived among them for nearly a year, slipping away to my 9-5 corporate job. I was surprised to discover the baseball fans. As the game progressed, single emotions would ripple down the bar—groans or cheers—until the crescendo moment when everyone broke ranks, backs were slapped, and I believed I saw a few tears. I left that bar with the feeling that anything was possible, that you could make up a 14-game deficit, that a small man could accomplish a big thing. Bus ticket in hand, I crossed the street.

There were two women seated in front of me on the bus. The little boy with them stood in the aisle. He had a baseball glove on his hand, and he was wearing a Boston Red Sox hat that looked just a little too large for his head. He had freckles. I guessed he was about eight years old.

I could only see the backs of the women's heads. The woman on my left hand, nearer the aisle, had brown curly hair with a kerchief on top. The woman on the window side of the seat also had brown hair, but it was totally straight, and redder than the other woman's hair.

The woman with the curly hair did most of the talking. She bobbed her head when she spoke, so that it almost seemed as if the thoughts were springing from the coiled launching pads of so many curls.

The other woman was younger. She looked to be in her late twenties or early thirties. The boy belonged to her.

"So you've never been to the city," the talkative woman said. "It's a great place," she promptly announced, "but you've got to keep your wits about you."

The younger head nodded.

The bus was moving through the greenery of upstate New York, on its way to the humming steadiness of the thruway, where only an occasional rock formation would break the visual monotony.

"You'll be arriving in the Port Authority," said the bobbing head. "Not a pretty place."

"We're only making a connection there," the young woman said.

"Oh," said the curly head. "So you're not really going to the city?"

"No," said the younger woman, but she didn't reveal her final destination.

"That's much worse."

"Why?"

"Because you'll be in that godforsaken Port Authority for who knows how long while you wait for your next bus …"

The boy was in his own world. He was rocking back and forth on the balls of his feet and humming to himself. He seemed to have made a game out of exaggerating the movements of the bus, as if they occasionally threatened to throw him to the floor. He would swing around and right himself, conquering every imaginary curve.

"Yes, it's a crazy place the Big Apple. No telling who's walking around, especially when it gets dark."

The younger woman nodded, but didn't say anything.

There was a long silence, in which I thought the older woman might have fallen asleep. We were making very good time. Traffic was surprisingly light. Soon the skyline came into sight. Soon the buildings burst into existence all around us.

The curly head shook itself and the familiar voice repeated its cautions all over again, more vehemently the deeper we made our way into the heart of the city.

"Now, remember," she said "you have to be careful. You don't know who you're dealing with. It's New York. You have to be very careful."

"Yeah," the boy with the Red Sox hat said in a surprisingly loud voice. "All those Yankee fans!"

Doorman

The uniformed doorman is an urban creature.

His habitat is the lobby of the high-rise apartment building, the squares of pavement directly in front of the building door, and the strip of street at the edge of that pavement, where he can sometimes be observed hailing a yellow cab.

His biological function is to be the consummate surrogate. He is the surrogate husband, there to ease the burden of wives who arrive home overloaded with packages. He is the surrogate friend, tireless conversationalist to the loneliest city dweller. He is the surrogate son to the elderly, recipient of their complaints and the occasional baked specialty. He is the watchful, surrogate father to the children who wander through his lobby.

Our doorman, Jim, took his job very seriously. We were young couples for the most part in a building recently turned co-op with fifty-two units and not a single child. Ours was not a rich building; we could only afford the services of a doorman from 4 o'clock in the afternoon until midnight.

One day William arrived, the building's first child. We treated him with a sense of continual wonder and amusement, as if we just could not get used to the appearance of such small child in such a large city.

William grew into a curly-haired kid with endless energy. It was not until he reached the age of four that the building's second child, Melissa, was born.

One day, Melissa's mother asked Jim to please keep an eye on the sleeping baby in the stroller while she went upstairs to get something. William suddenly appeared in the lobby, as he often did while Jim was on duty. Jim put his finger to his lips and gestured towards the baby.

William let out a screech and went running through the lobby.

"William, be quiet," Jim whispered sternly, gesturing again towards the baby.

William responded by shouting at the top of his lungs, running into the walls, jumping up and down, and shouting again and again.

"William, shut up!" Jim said.

William turned and said: "F—k you, Jim."

The tsunami begins as an underwater earthquake. Of course, Jim had heard these words before. But emerging from the mouth of a four-year old child they hit him like a wall of water 100 feet high.

Red-faced, Jim walked to the intercom and pressed one of the buttons. When the voice of William's mother came on, he said, "Mary, please come down here. We have to talk."

It was late in the afternoon, but clearly this was her first sortie of the day. She had on a housedress and slippers. She was wearing very large glasses.

"Mary, you can see Melissa's sleeping over there," Jim said, pointing to the baby, who, despite all of the noise, had not wakened.

"I asked William nicely to be quiet. He continued to make noise. I asked him again, and he made even more noise. So I said 'Shut up, William!' and do you know what he said to me?"

Jim paused ever so slightly. "He said, 'F—k you, Jim!'"

Mary looked at him, while his face alternated between one shade of red and another.

"Well, Jim," she explained, "we never say shut up in our house."

The Clock

We had been married for nearly a year. We were living in a large, one bedroom apartment on the west side. It had been my bachelor pad. One of the first items we had bought together was a very large, Howard Miller clock. It was completely round, three feet in diameter. It looked like a giant's pocket watch without the chain. We put it on the wall right above the dining room table where it became a great conversation piece.

An old friend of mine and his wife and two children were scheduled to visit one Sunday. We knew his wife, but we'd never seen the children, having fallen out of touch. Although I had a nephew and a niece we saw on many family occasions, we weren't quite used to the behavior of very young children. We were so unused to it that we didn't even know there was anything we didn't know. We thought of children as smaller adults, with special needs for sure, but we didn't think past that, except to know that we wanted some of our own very soon.

When the doorbell rang, we were greeted by my friend's wife. He remained standing against the back of the hallway, holding the two children, one in his arms, and one by the hand. After saying hello to us, she looked back at him and said, "Wait there while I check it out."

She moved deftly past us into the living room where she reconnoitered the situation like an advance soldier in the field. A bookshelf filled one of our walls. Interspersed among the books were many small items, figurines and other objects we had picked up in our travels, separately and together.

She zeroed in on the lower shelves and announced methodically to herself in a voice that we could hear: "This has to move. This can't stay here. This won't survive." As she spoke, she moved the objects higher on the shelves, out of the reach of small hands. Then she stepped back and surveyed the entire room. She found a few other items that needed rescue and placed them carefully in higher, parallel positions where she felt they would be safe. Then she turned to us with a smile, and said: "All clear." She opened the door and we heard her deliver the same message in the hallway: "All clear."

Two attractive boys came bouncing into the room—one walked and the other crawled. They followed the same paths their mother had just covered, but with pronounced impatience and rapid head movements. They were looking for something, but they wouldn't know what it was until they found it.

The wise mother opened a bag that we had not noticed until then, and began to spread brightly colored plastic toys in strategic positions around the room. The younger boy went straight to them. The older one continued to look around the room, but then finally sat down, bringing himself to the level of his crawling brother. We suddenly realized that we had not moved from our positions, standing together, since she had entered the room.

Then we remembered that we were the hosts and broke out the white wine and the hors d'oeuvres, and began the conversation.

"You'll understand all of that better," she said to us, using a phrase we had heard so often from our own parents, "when you have children of your own.

"They're very active," she said. "At this stage they hear voices that tell them to destroy anything they can reach."

The boys did not destroy anything. The conversation called up old times, college days, shuttling back and forth to the present. It covered jobs, the current political climate, personal histories, career choices, and there were a lot of questions from my wife about being a parent.

Eventually, we moved to the dining room, where my wife succeeded famously in delivering one of her first semi-formal dinners. Everything was perfect, except one part of the conversation.

The table was as round as the clock on the wall. I sat beneath the clock and directly across from me sat the younger boy, next to his mother, in a special seat that they had brought for him. It attached to the table in an ingenious way.

Wherever the conversation roamed, and it went many places, he kept looking at me and repeating the same sentence with the insistence of a child, over and over and over: "You have a big clock!"

But he was very young, and he couldn't make the sound for the letter "L."

Father-in-Law

It was a large room, but never had we seen it so full of people. In this room, lunches and dinners happened all the time, with a restful view onto the sloping green carpet of the golf course. In the winter, when the trees were leafless, as they were now, you could see the city skyline from certain tables. Weddings and anniversaries were celebrated here. So were company parties. Just last week, a christening had taken place. But none of these events filled the room as completely as today's memorial service.

There were nine scheduled speakers, beginning with the young man's daughters. Fifty is young. Fifty is the prime of life. At fifty, a man can find himself at the heart of a web of living relationships: son, brother, husband, father, friend, colleague, boss. A charismatic personality with a quick wit and a famous sense of humor could fill a room like this one. The room was overflowing.

The daughters recounted their memories, each one like a brightly colored shell found again on the silent shore. The friends of all ages rushed forward with bright moments that revealed the man, like lightning bugs in a jar. The office colleagues displayed portraits in which the figure in the painting winked slyly, his part in a conspiracy of humanity. The very good friend from way back made a moving speech, ending with an image from an anonymous poem, in which the sailor sets out across a great body of water, his white sail slowly becoming a speck to those standing on the shore, each thinking *there he goes*, but on another shore, the sail grows larger, and people are shouting, *here he comes*. There were no dry eyes in the room.

When the last speaker had finished, they asked whether anyone else wanted to say something. An older man stood up, and made his way to the microphone. First, he said, "I have a bet with my wife that I will make it all the way through this," and then he said, "I am the father-in-law.

"So many of you have said such nice things about Mark. I agree with you all, and I thank you. But, you know, no one has mentioned that Mark broke a lot of things, or I should say that things got broken when Mark was around.

"I remember the first time that he slept at our house. We set up a cot for him in the basement. Now, he was courting my daughter, so I knew I had to sleep lightly and remain vigilant. In the middle of the night, I heard him coming up the stairs, so I left my room to meet him. He said to me, "Sir, did you know that your water heater was broken?"

"'What do you mean,' I said to him, 'it's broken? How did it break?'"

"Another time, Mark was watching a football game at our house and we had an old-fashioned television set back then, with an antenna. When I came into the room, the picture was terrible."

"'What happened?' I said."

"'The antenna broke,' he answered."

"'By itself?' I wondered."

"Then there was the new car with a bent fender in the first week. Nobody knew how it happened, and recently, on the golf course, somehow the club got wrapped around the ball cleaner, and the shaft and the head got separated.

"Mark handed me both pieces and said, 'If you can get these together, you'll have a fine club.' Things just got broken.

"He was a great guy. I loved him like the son he became for me. And today, he leaves us all with broken hearts."

Snow

It had been a snowy winter. On this day, the sky was clear, the sun was out. I was on a short mission to deliver an envelope to my in-laws. No one was expected to be home. My plan was to drop my package at their door and return to the highway.

When I arrived, there was no one in sight. The entire neighborhood seemed to be sleeping. I parked and walked up to the doorway. The envelope fit neatly into the mailbox. As I turned to leave, I noticed that all of the sidewalks had been cleared except theirs. A thin layer of snow, no more than an inch high, covered their walkway.

"How long could it take?" I said to myself. So I walked over to the garage where I knew I would find the snow shovel and began to undertake what I thought would be a very quick, small gesture.

As soon as the shovel hit the snow, I realized how little snow there was—only a thin veneer on top of a sheet of ice. I persisted, thinking that this was only one small patch of ice. It wasn't. By moving down the walkway with the shovel, I uncovered a thick, uniform layer of ice.

"Now that I've cleared the snow," I thought, "what happens if someone slips on the ice?"

There had been footprints on the snow I shoveled.

I walked back to the garage and searched for an ice chopper. I found it soon enough, and made my way back to the walkway. I began chopping wedges and triangles of all shapes. It took some effort. I wanted to make sure to get all of the ice without chipping the concrete of the sidewalk underneath.

It took me about an hour to get everything done, except a certain patch under the shadow cast by a tree. The sun had not softened this six-foot long patch of ice. It defied the chopper. Instead of breaking through, I could only make dents marked by slanted white lines in all directions.

"Maybe I can leave this part," I thought. "People can just walk around it."

I looked down the length of the walkway. It was getting hotter. I began to wonder if the movement of the sun would have completed the entire job by itself a few hours from now much better than I ever could.

"What if the owner of one of those sets of footprints, seeing a clear pathway ahead, did not notice the only remaining patch of ice under the tree, and took a spill? Then clearing away the snow would have actually made things worse."

I took the chopper back to the ice and worked it over for another hour or so, until the walkway was clear.

Now I surveyed the property with a feeling of accomplishment, the way I used to do as a boy, holding my snow shovel. Then I noticed that the area right in front of the doorway was still untouched.

"Passersby had a clear path, but how ironic would it be if my own relatives or one of their visitors slipped on the ice going into or coming out of the house? People carry bags of groceries and other packages. They don't always look where they're stepping."

I brought the shovel and the chopper over to the doorway and got to work. I didn't stop until nothing was left undone. Now, I began to hope that someone would walk by. I hadn't seen a single person all afternoon.

I got in the car and turned on the radio. Beneath the static, I heard the voice of a general announcing that he expected the campaign to be quick and decisive, and the peace to follow in short order.

Windy Day

It was a windy day. My sister-in-law, who hardly ever asks anyone for anything, had a question. Would I mind going down to get the baby's stroller from the car? We were at a crowded family event. Her husband was not present. The baby had fallen asleep uncomfortably in one of the chairs.

She handed me the valet ticket. The parking lot was a sea of cars. Since most of the guests at the three simultaneous events happening in this large building had already arrived, and none were about to leave yet, finding a valet attendant was no easy task.

It was autumn and the fallen leaves were swirling up and down in crazy circular motions, driven by the wind. I walked into the small key house, where what seemed like a thousand sets of keys were on the wall. I tried to match the numbers on the valet ticket with one of the sets of keys, but the numbering systems were entirely different. Maybe this was a safety measure designed to prevent keys from falling into the wrong hands. Still, I couldn't imagine valet training that included matching and breaking codes, especially in the heat of the pick-up, when every driver seems on edge.

I stepped out of the key house. The wind blew in my face as I stared down one endless row of cars searching for the attendant. I turned the other way and looked again at the sea. This is how Napoleon must have felt reviewing his troops—row upon row at silent attention, waiting for the next command that would take them who knows where.

I remembered living on Riverside Drive where the wind was as wicked on certain days as anywhere else on earth. Businessmen joked about spending the day plastered to the sides of their buildings, briefcase at arm's length, unable to break away.

I thought I saw a lone attendant making his way towards me like a shepherd on the hill, growing slightly larger as he approached. He was certainly not in a rush.

He didn't speak much English. I had a difficult time explaining that I wanted the keys but not the car; that I wanted to know where the car was but I didn't want to take it away. Eventually I thought I got through. He handed me the keys.

Now I had to explain that I did not know where the car was. This problem was compounded by the fact that my sister-in-law had a new car, which I had never seen. I had to get close enough to see what was inside the car to identify it. I should have thought of this when I accepted the mission. I suppose I expected to just hand in the ticket and be presented with the car.

Instead we walked, as if through the countryside. He was my guide. As we walked, I began to wonder how the valets themselves located the right car. I concluded that it had something to do with where the keys were located on that massive board. When we did arrive at the car, I had to explain all over again that I did not want the car, but something inside of it. He threw up his hands and left me there.

I brought the stroller out, de-collapsed it, and rolled it towards the key house. As I passed the house on the way to the entrance to the hall, the attendant appeared gesticulating wildly. He wanted the keys back, which made perfect sense. I let go of the stroller to reach inside my pocket. At this moment, the wind blew the empty stroller away from me, through the gate, and into the traffic.

A passerby, seeing the baby stroller out of control and heading towards the oncoming cars, left his own family and dove into the street to retrieve it. Cars screeched to a halt. People gasped.

No one was hurt, but I thought I might be when he discovered that there was no baby in the baby stroller. I thanked him again and again and again, while I kept thinking, "He risked his life for nothing."

When I rolled the stroller out of the elevator, I saw my sister-in-law, standing there.

"Oh, thanks anyway," she said. "The baby woke up. What took so long?"

The Assignment

We found out about the assignment at the eleventh hour. He needed ten photographs of himself as a baby and a young child. Could he go through the photo albums and get some pictures?

"When is the assignment due?"

"It's due tomorrow morning."

"Why are you only telling us about it now?"

No answer.

We gave the usual lecture about not waiting until the last moment to start an assignment. And then we gave a new lecture about how important these pictures were to us, how in most cases we had only one copy, and how his telling us about the assignment so late made it impossible for us to make copies.

"I could have scanned them in," I said. "You could have made them part of the actual document, instead of messing with tape."

"They don't want us to do that," he said, impatiently. "Can I go through the books?"

We went through the books with him. He tolerated us. We had to admit that we enjoyed going through the books of photos. We didn't realize how much we had forgotten, not just the images in the photos, but the feelings that went with them.

We began to feel grateful for the assignment. We realized that we carried these feelings around with us all the time in a fuzzy way. Seeing the images allowed us to externalize them; the photos absorbed the feelings, making us feel lighter; it was a kind of catharsis.

He disappeared to the computer in the basement to complete his work, silently. He didn't show the final product. Somehow, he had become a child who never needed help with anything, except when he needed some physical thing over which we were the guardians, like the photographs.

In the morning, we impressed upon him once again the value of the photographs to us.

The last two months of the school year flew by. There were traveling games, parties, movies, tests, recitals, sleepovers, doctor visits, dances, new assignments, and what seemed like hundreds of rushed car trips to critical places always in the nick of time.

In the last few days of school, it occurred to us to ask about the photographs.

By the latest count, human beings have traversed the earth for 150,000 years. For most of this time, there were no photographs. The cavemen raised their young; and these young grew and raised their own young, generation upon generation, and never a single snapshot.

"Where are the photographs we gave you?"

No answer. And then …"I might have thrown them away … accidentally," he added quickly. "When I cleaned out my locker. Why is it such a big deal?"

The claw of the bear hit me on the side of the head. I fell against the rocks. It was all I could do to escape with my life. I would return from the hunt with nothing, except a feeling of emptiness that would last for days.

We lived through this feeling. We explored it. It taught us that these images were ours, not his, even though it was himself they pictured. We could not make them matter to him, the way they did to us.

Is growing up the process of throwing away the earlier images that parents preserve like the curators of a private museum? Was it our assignment to learn this?

If so, then we would have to find a way to feel good that we had completed it so early.

Aunt Jean

Aunt Jean is my godmother. She reminds me of this every time I see her. In vivid detail, she recounts how she and my godfather, Uncle Angelo, carried me through the streets of Brooklyn on the day of my christening. "We had no cars then," she always says, and I look down and see the cobblestones as if they are there right now, beneath my feet.

Aunt Jean is a character. She makes friends easily. Strangers warm up to her. She can be loud and uninhibited in the most positive ways. She loosens up the crowd. Everyone loves her.

Uncle Angelo was quieter. He loved sports and gambling for small stakes. He excelled at games of skill, like pool and bocce. He loved anything that involved a ball or a horse. He was a fan of the races.

He also loved the Yankees. He knew about every player going seven decades back. He spoke often about DiMaggio and Mantle and Maris, about Reggie and his favorite pitcher, Guidry, which he pronounced, "Jid-dree," softening the sound of the G.

He expressed the intense desire to meet, just once, Yogi and Rizzutto. Both men live only towns away from me, and I had met them separately at different times in public forums. It is one of my great regrets that I never devised a way to make this meeting happen for my uncle.

He was a fan with longevity. The players of each period were alive in his mind, each in their prime, getting the game-winning hit, making the impossible catch, striking out the side.

In what would turn out to be the last week of his life, before a scheduled operation, I see him gallantly showing my aunt some of the things she might need to know, like how to pump gas at the self-service station, something she has never done before. It is the ultimate act of chivalry. At age 84, he patiently stands there, full head of white hair, as she completes the task under his supervision.

Aunt Jean has always been an early riser. For years, she has called us every Saturday morning. Her call announces the day. If I pick up, she talks briefly with me. She expresses concern about my work, and then moves to my wife for the week's conversation.

Aunt Jean has never been a sports fan. Her only sport was shopping, bargain hunting to be more exact. It was rumored that she bought and stocked items in multiples and kept them for years. People said her basement resembled a warehouse. At one of the department stores where she worked, the manager would ask her for certain items from her inventory to fill the shelves on thin days.

I wish I could do more for my godmother. I know she's lonely. But she's also fiercely independent. I've invited her to come and stay with us. I've offered to drive out to pick her up, to take her anywhere she might want to go.

Here's how she changes the subject: "What do you think of the Yanks' chances this year? Is it going to happen?"

or "Will they ever give Jeter the MVP? At least Phil's in the Hall of Fame."

I think it's her way of letting me know that she's not really so alone.

Any day now, I expect her to tell me about the most accomplished single season in pitching history: "25 wins, only 3 losses. 19 strikeouts in one game. Jid-dree! Louisiana Lightning!"

My Lunch Date

I was about to have lunch with a breathtaking redhead many years my junior. We had known each other for nine years now, but each time we sat down together I learned something new about her.

"There's almost nobody here," she said. It was nearly three o'clock, late for lunch. "And we like it that way, right?"

"Yes," I said. It was a cut above the usual quick eating place. They served sandwiches and bagels of all kinds. The coffee was good. I took a sip.

Before me on the plate, was an "everything" bagel, with every kind of topping. It had real butter and two slices of Swiss cheese, something I knew I shouldn't be eating, but the combination of butter, cheese and bread transported me back, as I knew it would, to the part of my youth I had spent in Paris, walking on the wide boulevards, holding a loaf of French bread, similarly garnished. In the French shops, you could choose from a bewildering variety of cheeses, more it seemed, than any human could track or comprehend.

"What other things do we both like?" she said.

"We both like peaches and plums," I said.

"And we both like chocolate licorice," she said. "Mommy likes red licorice," she added.

"Red is okay," I said, "but I like brown licorice better. I also like black licorice," I said.

"I don't," she said. "Doesn't it sound like licorice should have liquor in it?" she asked.

"Yes," I said. "A little bit of liquor, not a lot, because it is only liquor-ish."

"Like ticklish," she said.

"Except ticklish means you're a lot ticklish, not just a little," I said.

The cheeses were arranged in a glass counter facing the patrons. The inside of the glass had a light that must have been on a timer, because at that moment it went out.

"Hey, that light went out," she said.

"That's so the cheeses can get some sleep," I said. "So they'll be themselves tomorrow. If they're not themselves, then the man making the sandwiches will pick up one cheese and it won't be itself. It will be another one, and he won't even know it."

Then she asked: "Does cheese want to be eaten?"

I rapidly scanned all of my reading of all of the philosophies stored in my brain. When in doubt, go back to the Greeks. They saw the world with new eyes, and faced the fundamental questions without fear. This time, I'd have to call on the help of the pre-Socratics. Everything participates in being. Changes in form are insubstantial. The cheese becomes something else, but that is only illusory, because it still participates in being. That's fine, unless you're the cheese. A moment ago you were, and now you're not—a cheese, anyway. It was a dilemma that could not be resolved.

She saved me by changing the subject.

"What's in soda?" she asked. She was holding her bottle of clear grape soda.

"It's mostly sugar and water," I said.

"What if the ocean had sugar in it instead of salt?" she asked. "Then when you got wiped out it would just taste good."

Two young women, at least twice her age, came through the door. Involuntarily, I looked up. I glanced at their faces and their clothes, the presentation of themselves to the world. I felt myself falling into a state where, while it lasted, I would see the beauty in everything, as I did in these two young women approaching us, walking past us, turning around as they made their selections in front of the cheese counter where the light had mysteriously come back on.

It flickered through my mind that in a future restaurant, someone sitting at a table would be taken by the beauty of this young girl, my daughter. It was as inevitable as the sunrise.

"Let's go home," she said.

"Do you want to go to the bookstore?" I asked. It was on the other side of the plaza.

"Okay," she said. We passed a bicycle leaning against the side of a brick building. It was probably used for deliveries of some kind. I couldn't get over its beauty and dignity. Its silence. Its usefulness.

We walked past the train station.

"I like train stations," I said. The name of the station appeared in white letters on a black background, announcing itself, staking its place in the railroad network. The parking spots, in short supply during the commuter week, lavishly offered themselves.

"I've never been on a train," she said.

"You're kidding," I said, incredulously. I went over all of the family trips we had taken—the five of us. She was our youngest. I guess none of them in her short life had involved a train.

"I want to show you something," I said.

We walked to the back of the parking lot next to the bookstore, and hidden away, beyond the very corner, there was a baseball field. Here it was, right in the middle of town, but you could not see it from any of the streets. Like the bicycle and the train station, it silently persisted in being itself. Off to the side, what had once been a bright orange tractor stood, its colors softened by the weather and the history of its existence.

Inside the bookstore, she decided that she wanted a certain pen in the shape of a vegetable. There were carrots, peppers, baby corns, eggplants … she chose a pod of peas. She practiced writing a squiggly line on a piece of paper offered by the clerk, and the sale was made. As we walked the length of the store towards the exit, surrounded by books on all sides, I thought, "Can there be any enterprise more optimistic than this—to write a book?"

"Well," I said. "I know what we're going to do next time."

"What?" she asked.

"We're taking a train ride."

Typewriter

Our middle daughter, aware of the family computer since infancy, asked me one day: "Daddy, did you know you can play solitaire with cards?" She was six at the time.

It reminded me of the day my nephew recounted the highlights of a game he had just watched on television. "Was it on cable or regular TV?" I asked.

"What do you mean?" he responded.

One Saturday afternoon, my youngest daughter and I went to visit my office. Everyone else in the family was out for the day, so we were left to take care of each other. Like her older sister, she had always found the computer to be very entertaining, so I thought it would please her to use one of our newest systems, which I had carefully detached from the network without disabling the internet, so she could visit dollzmania, nickelodeon, and any of the other websites where she spent time.

This is a fast box that can do remarkable things. I had linked the digital camera to it, and a new color printer. I planned to show her how by pressing one button we could transfer the pictures to the computer screen, and then print them out in full color on glossy paper. But she was far more fascinated by another machine.

The previous tenant had left behind a typewriter. She had never seen one before.

It thrilled her to press a letter of the alphabet and see the mechanical imprint it made right on the paper. Compared to the simulated voices and other sounds produced by the software programs she played every day, the sound of each metallic keystroke pleased her to no end.

"I'm going to write a story," she said, and set about typing the story of her life. It filled a little more than half of the page. It began with her birth and ended with a description of how much she loved our dog, Jack. In the middle she mentioned her mother, her "silly" father, and her two "sibblings." The story was funny and creative, especially the spelling.

After that, she decided to make her Christmas list, a single-minded use of time in the month of June. Here's how it went:

1. Typewriter
2. Typewriter
3. Type Writer
4. Typewriter
5. Typewriter
6. Typeriter
7. Typewriter, Typewriter
8. Typewriter
9. Typewriter Ribbins

I felt sure she would have her own typewriter before the leaves fell.

After I had read her story and her list, we walked down the stairs to get some fresh air.

"Is Mom home yet?" she asked.

"I don't know," I said.

"I want to call her."

"Okay," I said. "You can use my new cell phone. It's in the car."

She stopped walking and I stopped, too. She pointed to the phone booth across the street.

"I've never used a pay phone," she said.

Bicycle

My children have advised me several times that when given a choice of driving assignments—drop off or pick up—always be the drop off man. They explain that when you are bringing kids to a fun event they are in a good mood. When you come to take them away from the same event, usually back to their houses, they're going to be in a bad mood. "And they won't like you," they add, for emphasis.

This day, somehow, I found myself on the wrong side of the driving equation.

I parked the car in the school lot and made my way towards the gym where the dance should have been just coming to a close. Picking up is a tricky business for another reason. You have to arrive close enough to the end of the event that you won't be accused of spying, and early enough so you won't be considered late.

I entered at the back of the gym and joined the rest of the drivers. Male and female, we had the same look. We would have known each other anywhere, like pick pockets in a crowd, except that we were the crowd, the proud and reasonably happy members of the parent-servant class. We lived by unspoken rules, and one of those rules was you shall not look directly at the little children you had raised to see how they were faring, to observe how much they had grown, especially at a semi-adult event like a school dance.

You could, however, apply cunning. You could take off your jacket now that you were inside, and steal a glance as the disembodied sleeve passed before your eyes. You could get into a conversation with one of the mothers about anything and look briefly from time to time over her shoulder, talking all the while, searching for your offspring, and then return the favor by suddenly stepping out of some-one's way and in the process switching positions with her, so that she now had the high ground.

In one of these ways, I managed to find the astonishing woman my thirteen-year old daughter was becoming. She seemed happy out there on the dance floor and that made me happy. Then I scanned the room for another young girl, with whom I had barely ever spoken. I wanted to know that she, too, was dancing, and joyful, and happy to be alive.

Six years ago, I coached a baseball team made up of fourth and fifth grade boys. After a rocky start, the team really came together. The boys won ten games in a row, only to lose the final playoff game, a dramatic contest. On this particular day, we were still in the middle of the season. Kids who had begun slowly were now hitting the ball with authority. They were making sparkling plays in the field. I don't mind saying that I really looked forward to these games. On work-days filled with price negotiations and customer service calls, these baseball games offered me a clean, simple way to chart progress.

I had just turned the corner onto the tree-lined street in our town that would lead me to the field. I was constructing today's lineup in my mind when something in the periphery of my vision, something sensed before it was seen, made me slam on the brakes. It was a girl on a bicycle.

If it weren't such a worn phrase, I would say that she came out of nowhere. I think she came out of the driveway directly into the street, going at full speed, making a 90-degree turn right in front of my car.

The car did not hit the girl. The car did not hit the bicycle. The girl did not fall down. The bicycle fell. The round red reflector came off the bicycle, rolling in a diminishing circle until it fell, face up. The girl stood there, too shocked to move. Finally, I moved.

I got out of the car and stepped quickly to her.

"Are you alright?"

She nodded yes.

"Where did you come from?"

She didn't answer.

"Are you okay?" I repeated.

She nodded yes again.

"Do you want me to take you home?"

No response.

"I'll put your bike in the car."

She nodded no. A man walking a dog and a woman with a baby stroller both had stopped to look. I recognized the girl. She lived on this street, maybe ten houses down.

I bent down and picked up the bicycle, which I stood up, holding the seat. She put her hands on the grips.

"You're not going to ride it are you?" She was heading in the direction of her house. "Walk it home, on the sidewalk," I suggested. She moved to the sidewalk.

I got back in the car. I felt like less than a minute had passed. I drove very slowly towards the field, in the opposite direction of the girl with her bike.

Not two minutes later, I arrived at the field, where the boys were waiting for me, throwing around the one ball they had. The ice cream truck was parked, anticipating the start of the game, and the parents and younger siblings were beginning to gather. I popped open the trunk, which held the equipment, dialing my cell phone at the same time.

"Hello," I announced myself. "How is your daughter?" We weren't exactly friends, but we knew each other.

"Did you see it happen?" she asked. "My husband's out looking for a maniac hit-and-run driver."

"I'm the driver," I said.

"You!" she said, wanting to be angry, but sounding confused.

"I was going very slowly," I said. "Listen, I have a game to coach now, but I will drive over to your house as soon as it's over—about 8 o'clock."

I rang the bell later. The father, the mother, and the daughter were standing in the kitchen.

"Boy, did you scare me," I said to the little girl. "Where did you come from?"

"I rode into the middle of the street," she said. Her honesty moved me.

We had the expected exchanges about being careful, looking both ways, riding on the sidewalk, and just being happy that a tragedy had been averted. I left the house feeling greatly relieved, as if a tremendous amount had taken place in a short period of time.

Now, as the last notes of the last song announced the end of the dance, the kids moved towards the exit. The drivers and the driven found each other.

"Hi, Dad," my daughter said, moving her mouth but not her eyes, lest she be caught welcoming the enemy. Then I caught the eyes of the girl on the bicycle, now a young woman. We gave the slightest nod of recognition which held within it the shared memory of the event that did not change our lives forever.

Ice Cream

At the end of a particularly long day in the city, following three challenging meetings, one right after the other, I made my way to the train station. I arrived between trains. I had a wait of 24 minutes before the next train would leave.

I didn't feel like opening my laptop, or even thinking about anything having to do with work. I knew what I wanted to do. I wanted to read a book, so I walked over to the news corner, which had a collection of books on shelves in the back.

I needed something I could get into quickly. It shouldn't be too long either, because who knew when I would have the luxury of time to continue reading at the pace I expected to begin. It's not as if I take the train every day. I scanned the shelves.

After reading the first paragraphs of several paperbacks I settled upon a book of short stories. The cover identified the author as Europe's greatest storyteller. I had read some of her stories before, and I agreed that they were very good, perfect really for the train ride home.

As I stood on the line leading up to the cashier, my eye caught the freezer on wheels and suddenly I knew there was something else I needed—an ice cream bar ... chocolate on the outside, vanilla ice cream on the inside. I had to have it. I stepped out of the line and returned with both of my indulgences. The difficulties of the day began to dissolve.

I took my place on the bench in front of the gate that would lead to my train. To savor the moments ahead, I decided not too open either the book or the ice cream until I was sitting in the train.

Ten minutes later, I took my seat on the train. I opened the book and the ice cream. I read the first sentence of the first story and took the first bite. Then I heard crying.

I looked to my right towards the sound and I saw a boy maybe a year old, a year-and-a-half at most, standing on his mother's lap and pointing at my ice cream.

Here's how it made me feel. If I hadn't already opened it and taken that bite, I would have given it to him. The mother tried to distract him but the crying just got louder. I hid the ice cream behind the book and ate it more quickly than I wanted to with much less pleasure than I had anticipated. It was as if I was trying to destroy the evidence.

With the ice cream gone, I relaxed into the book. The story asked me to follow it down certain paths, which I did willingly, because I wanted to know what would happen next, and because the voice was consistent and attractive and alluring.

The family descended from the train.

One of our daughters was at camp and we took turns each night sending her e-mails about what was happening at home. Tonight I would tell her about the train, the book, the boy, and the ice cream.

The voice in the stories brought me forward like the movement of the train. I would tell my daughter about the difference between the ice cream and the book—that you could consume one of them in its entirety and still have the whole thing to give to someone else. This tiny observation carried me home.

Soap Opera

One day, when he was about two years old, my son and I crossed the street together just outside our city apartment and entered Riverside Park.

There were two paths you could take—one led downwards under the shade of elegant trees. Impressive rocks gathered in a cluster since a time before there were any buildings across the street or anywhere.

The upward path took you to a small field of grass and stone benches. Sunlight was everywhere. Beyond the wall, you could see the river and the buildings on the opposite shore.

I handed my son a yellow whiffle bat, and set him up on the edge of the field in the batter's position, with his back to the river. From a distance of five or six large steps away, I pitched a plastic ball underhand. He swung and missed. He was a little boy with a dark, incredibly curly head.

"Are you ready?" I said, and pitched the second ball. He swung and missed.

I walked over to him and gently took the bat from his hands.

"This way," I said, smoothly swinging the bat in one even motion. I handed the bat back to him.

I went back to my pitcher's position. I pitched the ball. He swung and missed. I pitched again. He swung and missed. Before each new pitch, I paused, and said: "Are you ready?"

After the twentieth pitch, he had still not made contact with the ball.

"Are you ready?" I said, and pitched again. This time he swung and the ball came rapidly back at me—a line drive that hit me in the upper chest and bounced away. I heard clapping and cheering.

I turned around to see five members of the cast of the soap opera *All My Children*, who had been watching us from the path. A white-haired actor stood in front of the group, leading the cheer.

Whenever I'm switching channels and see his face fill the screen, I stop long enough to find out what trouble he is wrestling with at that moment, and think back to this day.

Empathy

I knew my mother would pick up the phone. These days, my father has difficulty getting around. His pride won't let him use the walker the hospital provided when he was recovering from his broken hip. Instead, he moves slowly from one strategically positioned piece of furniture to the next. They are like stepping stones across a raging river.

As he made his way to the phone, I reflected on how much this day—Father's Day—has become Grandfather's Day.

"Hello," he said in a deep, unsteady voice.

"Happy Father's Day," I said.

"Well, same to you," he said. "How are the kids?"

"Everyone's fine."

"That's good, that's good," he said. "That's what matters."

The broken hip is not really what has slowed him down. It is the leukemia. At one point, he endured 27 blood transfusions in the space of 33 days. For nearly ten years now, his doctors have done a remarkable job of managing the disease.

I called because I knew we would not be seeing him today. The traffic and the distance between the two grandfathers make it impossible for us to see them both in the same day. We had visited my father last year.

My son does not want to go anywhere today. He would rather stay home with his friends. I explain that not going is not an option. He begins to sulk.

We reach a compromise. He and I will go later than everyone else in a separate car. We'll also leave earlier. He can make a respectful appearance without sacrificing the entire day.

Half an hour after my wife and the girls, we set out. He has his learner's permit now, so he takes the wheel. We need gas. Within a few miles of our departure, I scan today's prices at four stations very close to each other, and ask him to pull in at the one with the lowest price. While he has been driving with us for several months, it occurs to me that he has never pulled up to a gas pump.

I hand him my credit card and he gives it to the attendant. While we wait for the tank to be filled, I go over in my mind the conversation with my father this morning and wonder whether it matters to him that we will not see him this year on Father's Day.

There is a rapping at the window. I turn to see an old man's face inches from my own.

"What's this old guy want?" I say, before lowering the window.

"Can you do me a favor?" he asks.

I am expecting one of those stories about a series of unfortunate events leading up to a request for bus fare.

Instead, he hands me a card with his name on it.

"Mr. Harold Pines," I read aloud, looking at the card. There is no "Mister" there, and I'm not sure why I add it. Saying the name, I sound like Rod Serling at the beginning of a twilight zone episode.

He leans on two canes to keep his balance. His glasses are somewhat askew. He is unshaven. His pants are high and uneven. The belt is too big. He is dressed too warmly for this hot day.

"Can you call this number for me?" he asks. "I've been waiting for half an hour. Are they still coming?" It is an emergency road services card.

I look past him to see a dilapidated vehicle 20 yards away. It seems as if the axel is broken. The tire is completely off the rim.

I take my cell phone and step out of the car. I punch in the number on the card and get a voice message offering me several options. I follow the path for inquiring about incidents that have already been reported. The voice tells me: "All of our counselors are busy helping other customers. Please stay on the line. Your call is important to us. It will be picked up by the first counselor who is free." I hear this message a half-dozen times before I turn back to Mr. Pines who has an expectant look on his face.

I'm concerned that he has been standing too long and I motion him back to his car, where he can sit on the driver's side seat with the door open, above the wrecked wheel.

"The guy nearly hit me when I was coming in to the station," he said. "I had to swerve out of the way and I hit the pole." He pointed to a telephone pole. All the while, the voice in my ear kept telling me how important my call was and that a counselor would soon be helping me.

"He never stopped," Mr. Pines said. "He just kept driving."

I imagined the old man swerving out of the way and crashing into one of the gas pumps instead of the pole, with explosions to follow, and flames rocketing into the sky. The voice in my ear continued.

His car was full of junk, folded maps and food containers. I wondered if he had led an untidy life, or if it was just the entropy of old age that brought him to this state. I wondered if he had children and why they were not visiting him on Father's Day.

Once he was seated, I walked around the edge of the station looking for the attendant. The voice kept on promising the next counselor. I looked at my son in the driver's seat of our car. The tank had long since been filled. Twenty minutes had now passed.

I found the attendant, but he spoke no English. My thought was to get a second call going on the station phone, improving our chances for a connection. I pointed towards his phone and said, "It's an 800 number," but I was sure he didn't understand me.

I put the second call on the speaker, and then quickly walked back to Mr. Pines, who must have thought from my pace that I had news for him. I walked quickly so I could get back to the gas station phone in case someone picked up. I told him what I was doing, and ran back to the station phone. Forty minutes had now passed.

I was trying to come up with an alternative plan when Maria answered my cell phone.

"Maria, I've been on your line for more than half an hour. I'm trying to help an old guy. He can't walk, he can't hear, he can barely see. He's sitting in his disabled car waiting for your tow truck. His name is Mr. Herbert Pines (again, I said 'Mister') and this is his emergency services number." I read the number.

"You've really got to help this guy out. I've been on the line for forty minutes!"

"I'm sorry," she said. "There are only four of us here. It's Father's Day."

"What can we do for Mr. Pines, Maria?"

It struck me that the people we were on the way to visit might have concluded by now that my son had persuaded me not to go, after all.

I walked back to Mr. Pines to tell him that I had made contact with emergency road services. He stood up with difficulty and began searching through his pockets. I was hoping that he didn't think he had to give me money. I was relieved when said, "Did you give me my card back?" I had already given him the card.

Maria came back on the line to say that she could not get in touch with the towing company. No one was answering. But exactly at that moment, I was able to report to her that the tow truck had arrived. It had tremendously oversized wheels.

I looked at Mr. Pines who was in instant, deep conversation with the tow truck driver. He was showing his card, which the driver took in one hand. For an hour, he had become my old man. Now he belonged to the tow truck driver about to transport him to someone else. The Twilight Zone theme played in my head.

I walked towards the car where my son sat in the driver's seat, looking into the distance.

Saint Yogi

There are five Roman Catholic churches within a mile of our "new" house in the suburbs, but we didn't know this in the first week of our arrival, only days before Christmas. I put *new* in quotation marks because the house was built in 1908. None of these five churches, by the way, is in our town.

Snow was predicted upon our arrival. I moved the car to the end of the driveway. I didn't know if I would find a snow shovel in the garage, and by the time the weather bulletin appeared on the television, it was already dark. We came from the city and owned nothing as useful as a flashlight, so even if I wanted to search the garage for a shovel, I wouldn't be able to see anything.

It did snow the next morning, and it continued to snow for a few days, but lightly, just enough to reinforce the Christmas feeling.

On Christmas morning, we entered the first church we found. During the mass, when the priest exhorts the members of the congregation to give each other the sign of peace, I turned around to see our four-year old son shaking the hand of Yogi Berra, hall of fame catcher, local hero, and source of endless good sense.

That's how we came to choose our parish.

Garage Sale

My wife and I feel differently about things.

Nothing reminds me of this as vividly as our yearly garage sale.

The garage sale is almost entirely her production. For weeks in advance, she piles into the garage the things she has decided we no longer need. In the days leading up to the event, she runs an ad in the newspaper. The night before, she hand letters two signs for posting on the trees out front.

I have only one responsibility—to move the things from the garage to the front lawn. In so doing, I feel a certain nostalgia for these things, which is ironic, since I did not want most of them in the first place.

My wife regularly accuses me of not needing things. "My husband could live without running water," she says. This is an exaggeration. One of the things I can't live without is a hot shower in the morning.

What I think she means (and see how carefully I've chosen those words) is that because I do not seem to need things that other people require, I must think that they do not really need them either, and that she is one of those people.

As I carry them to the front lawn, I agree that we just do not need some of these things anymore, yet that does not lessen my attachment to them, especially if they are toys that were once loved. It bothers me that at one moment in time we would have done bodily harm in the pursuit of a ninja turtle, the next power ranger, or a certain video, and that now they lay lifeless in a pile on sale for a tiny fraction of their original cost. I think it does something invisible, but long lasting, to our psyches.

It also bothers me immensely that my wife has put out the four chairs that go with our claw-foot table, the first table we ever owned, in our city apartment. She must know, I thought, that parting with these items would be painful for me. She knew enough to carry them out by herself, at the last minute, from another location.

Looking at the chairs, I suddenly understand our different attachment to things, that she is attached to getting new things, while I am attached to keeping what we have. It flickers through my mind, like a brief flash of light, that she might discard me before I let go of her.

I return later in the day to find out that this year's garage sale has not been the success of previous years. Last year brought in more than $800, while this year the total is $250. I notice that the chairs are still there on the lawn.

I ruffle the dog's head playfully. He roams free, contained by the hidden electric fence. Today he was excited by all of the garage sale activity.

I wasn't so keen on getting the electric fence. Whenever the dog strays toward the edge of our property, he hears a high-pitched sound right before getting zapped. He learns that the sound is followed rapidly by the zap, and that's what keeps him in place.

I thought this was cruel and unusual punishment, but my wife explained to me that it was much less cruel than keeping him tied to the tree, which is what we were forced to do before.

In the first few days, he didn't know what hit him. Always anxious to get out of the house, the zapping turned him around. He became afraid of the outside world. He cowered in the house. He just didn't understand. This all took place in the week of that the Twin Towers came down.

Eventually, he came around, with the help of the trainers from the hidden fence company. He had never bolted through the fence enduring the electric pain to get at something on the other side, until today.

I was sitting in the kitchen when I heard something beyond barking. The sound was closer to what you might hear on the movie set of *Jurassic Park*. I ran down the driveway to see our dog on the other side of the hidden fence in mortal combat with a German shepherd. The owner of the other dog, a petite woman, was on the ground, entangled in both leashes while the dogs fought each other as if they were auditioning for parts in a suburban production of *Call of the Wild*.

The dogs were separated. The woman stood up, swearing that she was okay. The German shepherd seemed untouched. Our dog was bleeding heavily from the ear. I piled him in the car, and we drove to the animal hospital.

I had never been there. They took the patient from me, and ushered me to a room at the end of a long, sterile corridor, where I sat silently. I suddenly felt as if I was inside of a science fiction story. The doctor would come and operate on the corresponding part of the dog owner's body, and the animal would be cured. The doctor entered the room.

He was holding a clipboard. He explained to me that there were two options. Our first option was to wrap the ear. It would heal this way, but it would always be separated along the lines introduced by the German shepherd's teeth. It would most likely not get infected again. It would most likely not bleed again.

The second option would make the dog whole again. They would sew the ear back together. It would be as good as new. There would be no chance of infection. There would be no further bleeding. The cost of the second option was double the first. The second option would cost $500.

So I had to choose between a break-even day, in which the operation would cancel the garage sale, and a day in which one visitor to the garage sale would cost twice what it brought. Naturally, I chose the latter. I couldn't imagine having anyone, let alone my own kids, look at the dog and say oh yeah, he has a separated ear because my dad wouldn't pay to have it put back together.

Besides, I loved the dog now, even if I may not have wanted him in the beginning. I was attached to him, and I was attached to the idea of having the two parts of his ear attached.

When he left the hospital he had an inverted lamp shade on his head. This was so that he couldn't scratch the wound. He was crashing into things and having difficulty finding his bearings.

I arrived home in darkness. Before I brought him in to show the kids, whom I knew would beg me not to let him out while he had this thing on his head, I let him get used to the front lawn again, while I carried the remaining items from the day's sale back into the garage. In a day, I knew he would conclude that this lamp shade was something he would have to wear for the rest of his life, like the electric collar around his neck.

For now, he frolicked in the night air, prancing on either side of me as I took the four claw-foot chairs back into the house, one by one.

The Same Old Stuff

You can divide the people in our extended family into two types: the easy-going and the demanding. For whatever mysterious reason, these two types tend to find each other in marriage. This holds true throughout the family except in the case of one of my cousins. Anyone who knows her would have to agree that she and her husband, both high school teachers, fall into the easy-going category.

I should tell you that I am disposed towards easy-going people. The major complaint I have against the demanding ones is that they tend to be demanding of everyone else, but very easy-going on themselves. Nevertheless, I can see how an entirely easy-going household might be prone to chaotic moments.

My cousin and her husband were in the process of selling their house. They had three children now, and wanted a bigger place. Every weekday morning five people and a dog went through the haphazard motions of getting themselves ready for the day, except this morning was different. No one had kept very good track of the fact that the real estate broker would be arriving with a potential buyer.

One of the children was upset because something necessary for the school day could not be found. The dog was raising a ruckus, but no one was paying attention. My cousin patiently tried to help her child by looking in every conceivable place for the missing item. A horn honked outside announcing the twins' ride to school. In rapid succession, the two children ran out for their ride, the lost thing was found turning tears into smiles, the real estate broker appeared with her customer at the end of the driveway, and the dog, unable to contain himself any longer did his business on the kitchen floor.

Easy-going people don't panic outwardly. My cousin, seeing the real estate broker's car, stepped quickly through the kitchen only to be stopped dead in her tracks by what the dog, now cowering in the corner, had left behind.

The broker was giving the customer a tour of the grounds. They were reviewing the shrubbery when my cousin took the only action that came to mind. She put the offensive contents in a brown paper bag and hid it in the only place she felt sure it would not give off an odor during the brief, important visit about to take place. She put it in the refrigerator.

While the broker, the customer, and my cousin walked through bedrooms and the dining room, my cousin's husband came down the stairs in his jacket and tie, took his lunch from the refrigerator, and drove to work.

You can guess the rest of the story. But you may not know that the teachers at his school keep their lunches in the same refrigerator, and that they eat together in a common dining room.

They joke about having the same old same old every day for lunch.

On this day, this observation took on added poignancy as he opened and rapidly closed the brown paper bag on the table before him.

Most Valuable Player

My son asked me if it was possible to pray for something not to happen.

He was a seven-year old boy kneeling at the foot of his bed just learning how to say his prayers.

"Sure," I said. And then he prayed to God in his infinite mercy to prevent the 1994 major league baseball strike from continuing into the 1995 season. Then he turned to me and asked if I would coach his baseball team this year.

My team had boys and girls on it. This would be the first year they would face pitched balls, instead of hitting off the tee. Coaches pitched to their own teams. There was a guideline that if a child did not hit the ball in a certain number of pitches the tee should be brought out, but I paid no attention to it. As the pitcher-coach, I considered it my job to study each errant swing and aim the ball at the bat. We didn't use the tee once.

Before the first practice, I sat everyone down on the grass. From how they were holding their gloves, I saw that we would have to begin with basics, like the difference between right-handed and left-handed.

"How do we know which hand to put our gloves on?" I said.

"I know," one boy said, matter-of-factly. "It's the hand you don't color with."

There was a rule that you had to change everyone's position each inning, so that no player spent too much time in the outfield. This meant that the whole team would gather around me whenever we were about to take the field, each one begging for an infield position. It got so that I made one of my own rules—you could end up playing any position except the one you requested. It didn't take long for everyone to start asking to play the outfield.

I relented once. One of the boys jumped up and down, shouting, "I want to play shortstop! I want to play shortstop! Let me be shortstop!"

"Alright," I said. "Play shortstop."

"Where *is* that?" he asked.

Baseball at this level is a different game. An out is the rarest of things. There were two ways to retire the side—the traditional three outs, which almost never happened, and a complete run-through of the batting order. Runs were plentiful. So were overthrows, and misplays of every kind. It would have been more accurate to change the way scoring is kept by crediting a team with the number of outs it got in the field instead of the number of runs it scored. We didn't keep score, but so many runners crossed the plate that the members of both teams left each game convinced they had won.

We had other peculiarities. From time to time, I would find one of my players crying: standing in the outfield; in the on-deck circle with a batting helmet firmly in place; alone on the bench, curiously separate from the rest of the players. I always asked what might be wrong in an understanding tone. If the reason was something physical and minor, this was always a relief. But usually the source remained mysterious, even to the player, it seemed.

One boy threw his glove on top of the backstop once every game, while two others, full of energy, scrambled up the chain links in a race to retrieve it. These were sub-dramas, like the events happening in the corner of a painting by Breughel.

One player emerged.

If it's possible for a seven-year old to possess management skills, she did. First, she knew the game. She knew what a force play was, and not to leave the base when an infielder might catch a line drive or a pop-up. These were major achievements.

On this small playing field, she had mastered the fundamentals—she could hit, hit with power, run, throw and field—but her talents did not have so much to do with physical size or experience as they did with intense focus. In a game where no score was kept she became upset with herself and others whenever a performance could have been better. She would come to me with suggestions about re-positioning the players in the field. She willed perfection.

The crowning moment came in the last game. With runners on first and second, a ground ball was hit to her at shortstop. She fielded it cleanly, tagged the runner on second as he ran by, stepped on second base to force the runner on first, and then threw the ball to our shaky first baseman who caught it this time to complete the triple play—a remarkable outcome even at the major league level.

After the game, I carried the equipment to the car for the last time. I threw away the carton that held the new baseballs now that none were left. The kids were passing with their parents. They waved good-bye and I waved back. Some of them came forward to thank me, and I thanked them for a great season.

When she arrived, I told her and her father what a great player she was and what a great future she had. What I was really thinking was not the kind of thing I would say because it sounded too corny, too much like a self-help aphorism. Even mentioning the future seemed out of place.

Yet I wanted a seven-year old girl to know that the independence and the confidence she exuded was a precious gift that needed nurturing.

The season that had begun for me with a prayer was ending with a mantra, even if I could not say it out loud: *Be your own MVP.*

Altar Boy

I was in the last group of altar boys required to memorize the Mass in Latin and I was in the first group of Catholic High School students not required to study that language. Consequently, mysterious, ancient phrases inhabit my brain to this day.

The night before the first Mass I was scheduled to serve I could not sleep. My debut would take place in the convent at the early hour of 6AM for the nuns who had been my teachers and disciplinarians for the past six years. I had set my alarm for 5 o'clock, but I was plagued by fears that it would not go off, or worse, that I would sleep right through it. So I kept tossing and turning, looking at the faintly illuminated hands to assure myself that I had not missed the moment. I checked the clock what seemed like hundreds of times as the night crawled towards morning.

Then I must have fallen asleep, because I was jolted awake by the thought that the alarm clock had failed me. I stared across the bed and saw to my horror the hands on the clock telling me that it was a quarter to six. I jumped out of the bed. How could this have happened? I was waking forty-five minutes later than planned and only fifteen minutes before the Mass would take place.

There was no time to shower. I threw on my clothes. Out of the closet, I took the white surplice which my mother had ironed for me, handling it carefully despite my hurry, ran down the stairs and out to the garage where I found my bike in the darkness. I rode through the eerily quiet streets holding the surplice on its wire hanger behind me like a sail. I could feel beads of sweat on my brow. Involuntarily, I tried to manufacture meaningful excuses to explain away my lateness. I did not see a single person, and the only cars were parked and silent, like haystacks in a field.

Even though the words were in a language I did not know, they did not cause me as much worry as remembering all of the actions that had to take place, each at the right time—ringing the bells, raising the book, bringing the wine and water.

But what a luxury to be concerned about the performance itself! I raced through the streets wondering how much of the ceremony I had already missed.

When I arrived, I left my bike against the fence and quickly climbed the imposing steps to a large wooden door. I rang the bell and waited. No one came. I was torn between waiting and ringing the bell again. I did both. I waited, and when I could no longer wait, I rang the bell again.

I heard footsteps. The door creaked open. A tall, gray figure looked down at me. It was one of the sisters wearing a long, shapeless gown. I had never seen a nun without her black and white habit. She said not a word, but moved her hand slowly in my direction. She was wearing a large, men's watch. She brought the face closer and closer to mine. I was sure she was chastising me for my lateness, and I braced, but as the watch reached its full size, I saw that the time was a quarter to 4.

She shut the door and left me to puzzle out that when I had been shaken by the hands of my alarm clock—one on the six and one on the three—the time had actually been 3:30 and not 5:45.

As I rode home, the lightest mist formed in the air, rain before it becomes droplets, and the sweat that had just driven me in the opposite direction, was replaced by the refreshing sensation of this mist on my brow. It's a feeling that comes back whenever I almost forget there are second chances.

Meat Man

I got my first job when I was sixteen years old.

I had heard that one of the national all-purpose retail chains was hiring for the summer. The store was in a new strip mall some five miles from my house.

My father drove me down to fill out the application. He waited in the car while I did it. During the ride back to the house I told him that they would let me know about the application in a few days.

Two days later I was hired. I took the bus to work, arriving well before my start time. I had no idea what my duties would be. In the Deli Department, I met my new boss, Frank. He had on a white apron. His hair was slicked back. He wore a white cap that looked like it was taped to his hair.

This store sold everything, from clothes and stationery items to garden tools and appliances. Frank let me know that I was now a member of the Deli Department. He pointed to the long, glass counter through which the patrons could view the items we had to sell. One of my responsibilities, he explained, was to keep that glass free of fingerprints.

Frank then showed me what he called "the equipment." Like the proud captain of an artillery unit, he gave me the tour of three shiny meat slicers.

"You have to respect the equipment," Frank said, "or it won't respect you. Always use the safety guard. The equipment doesn't know your finger from a pepperoni. It will slice both just as cleanly."

He then gave me his lecture on weights and balances. He said that over time I would become better and better at estimating the weight of the customer's order.

Rule #1 was: "Never offer the customers less than what they order. If they ask for ½ pound of something, cut a little more. They'll always pay for the extra. It's America," he said, "everybody always wants more."

I was a very conscientious worker. I took the bus early. Sometimes I would arrive an hour before work, and start shining the glass right away.

Most of the customers were women. They usually had shopping carts overflowing with items of all kinds. There were crazy moments. The presence of three or four women waiting for their orders seemed to remind others just passing by that they needed something too. So a certain number of customers standing in front of the counter seemed to produce an even greater number of customers. At the same time, too many customers waiting would discourage passersby from joining the line.

In the glass counter, there were all kinds of meats and cheeses. There were eight salamis, bolognas of different brands, Swiss cheese, Muenster cheese, head cheese which I couldn't imagine eating, mortadella whose name seemed to imply that someone had died, turkey role, liverwurst, every kind of sandwich fixing you could imagine, and many of each item.

In the frenzy produced by an overflow of customers, we would slice the salami and then toss it back into the glass counter, slice the bologna and toss it back into the glass counter. When the next person asked for salami, you'd see one of us searching for the salami in the counter. Once you found it, you'd slice and send it back. And then take the next order.

At the beginning of my second week of work, on the sixth day to be exact, after I had finished shining the glass counter, and feeling the kind of camaraderie that developed on the battlefield, I approached my commanding officer.

"I have an idea, Frank," I said. "Why don't we keep all of the meats in the same place all the time? If we cut a salami, we could always return it to the same place with the other salamis. When the next person asks for salami, we'll know exactly where to go for it and it will save time."

Frank looked down at me. Until now, I had never realized how tall he was—well over six feet. He looked directly at me with an odd expression on his face. He said, "Don't think this job is going to be that easy."

The day passed in the usual way, with the usual frenzy. When I reported to work the next morning, Frank took me aside. He told me that there had been oversight in personnel. They had actually hired too many people, and since I was the last one in, I had to be the one to go. He was sorry about it, but there was nothing he could do. I could pick up my check in the office.

I didn't go home right away. I was trying to figure out how to tell my parents about this turn of events. They had seemed overly happy when I got the job. How could I explain to them that I had lost it just a week later?

I walked up and down the strip mall. I couldn't buy or do anything. Free lunch was one of the benefits of working in the Deli Department. I only had the money for the return trip by bus and a check, but no bank account.

Somehow I stretched out the day, and arrived home at the usual time. After a few hours, I got myself to deliver the news. Immediately, I could see the look of concern on my parents' faces. Their oldest son could not hold down a job. "What did you do?" my mother asked.

My father recovered first. He said, "Look. You have experience now. You're a meat man. There are plenty of jobs in your line of work. Let's start with the nearest deli."

We got into the car together. Three blocks from the house, on the main avenue, there was an Italian delicatessen. We parked outside. I went in alone. The place was full of customers. Cheeses and strings of garlic hung from the ceiling. There were four guys behind the counter in a very small space. They seemed to be falling over each other as they filled the orders.

I got the attention of one of them. He came over to me wiping his hands on his apron.

I said: "I'm a meat man. I have experience. I was wondering if you had any openings."

"Oh no," he said. "Not right now," and then he said, "Wait a minute." He went back behind the counter and began talking to one of the other guys, and gesturing towards me. They were a type, this pair. They looked like Abbott and Costello. The one who had spoken to me was Costello.

He came back and said, "Can you start today?"

I went out to the car to tell my father that I was starting right away. "You are?" he said, as if he hadn't really believed his own encouraging advice. I told him I'd be home later.

I worked most days after school and every summer through high school in this place and even during holidays my first year at college, until the day when, distracted by the young woman standing in front of me, I sliced off the tip of my finger. "It happens to all of us," one of my bosses explained.

The Little Things

The other day I opened the old roll-top desk. I was looking for any pictures of the family that might have escaped our photo albums. Our son is graduating from high school this year and parents have been encouraged to submit early photos to the yearbook project. I found some of them. They succeeded in transporting me back in time. But so did some other objects in the desk. In one of the drawers I found metal subway tokens, made obsolete by the introduction of the paper metro card. The feel of them in my hands had the same power as the photographs.

Back then, I had my office in a brownstone on the Upper West Side of Manhattan. As the company grew, we filled more and more of the building's space, so that eventually we occupied three floors. There was a painting on the ceiling of the second floor that could be seen from street level through the bay window. It depicted two angels reaching out to each other, on a background dramatic with clouds and blue sky.

This office was a quick walk from our apartment. Although I owned a car, it spent most of its time idle in the parking garage. I took the subway to most of my meetings, located in different parts of the city. The last three times I had arrived at the token booth just as the train pulled into the station. While I hurriedly collected my change from the agent, I watched the train leave without me. Then I looked at my watch to assess whether the next train might get me to my meeting on time.

On this particular morning, I resolved not to get caught short-handed again. Even though my meeting would not take place until late afternoon, I began my morning by walking to the subway to purchase two tokens. I joined the line of anxious commuters, but instead of spinning around and heading for the turnstile, I pocketed my tokens, like a squirrel with an acorn and a plan. I fought my way up the stairway, against the tide, and made my way to the office at a leisurely pace.

I took off my coat. I was wearing a blue blazer with gold-colored buttons, the most standard of men's jackets. After lunch, my accountant arrived and we sat across from each other at the round table with stacks of paper in front of us.

At one point, he got up to go to the men's room. I glanced at the clock and realized that if I didn't leave at that moment, I might be late for my meeting. I wrote a quick note to say that I had to leave, but that we would talk during the week. I put on the blazer, left behind the coat because the sun was shining brightly, and headed to the subway.

As I came down the stairs I saw the train pulling into the station. With a slow display of confidence, I reached into my pocket for one of the tokens. My pocket was empty. I put the other hand in the other pocket; it, too, was empty. I checked my pants, thinking I might have transferred the tokens without realizing it. Nothing.

Then I thought: that must have been yesterday when I bought the tokens. I'm really slipping. It was a little thing, and I decided that it had no meaning. I would pay no attention to it. I bought two tokens and took a spot on the other side of the turnstile, checking my watch to see what chance I had to make the meeting on time.

Everything went well during the meeting. Since I arrived back after 5 PM, I went straight home. It was Friday. When I returned to the office on Monday morning, I discovered that the accountant had scribbled a message for me in black magic marker, across the note I had left for him.

It said: "You stole my jacket!"

I went straight to the office closet, where I found my blazer, with two tokens in one of the pockets.

Swing Set

When real estate agents showed us possible houses in possible neighborhoods in the suburbs we silently counted swing sets. We had a four-year old and a one-year old at the time, and we wanted to be sure that we were moving to a kid-friendly part of the world. Swing sets were our benchmark.

We didn't get our own swing set until we had lived in the house for a year. I arrived home from work one day just as the assembly team had finally put all of the pieces in place. It was an impressive structure, looming large, lacking only a red warning light at the top for passing aircraft.

One afternoon, I was swinging both kids at once. My wife was planting flowers. A sudden, loud sound came out of the distance. Involuntarily, I looked up, and in that moment my son's swing hit me square in the upper chest. Miraculously, he bounced off of me, barely deterred on his swinging path. My wife turned back from the loud sound to see me holding my chest, like a heart-attack victim, and said, emphatically, "Don't leave me with two kids!"

Discovering so many swing sets helped us choose our new neighborhood. The beech tree out front helped us pick our house. It was majestic, with reddish leaves and thick bark that looked like elephant skin. The massive roots springing out of the trunk resembled elephants' feet. No one visited the house without commenting on the beauty and expansiveness of the tree.

One day we got bad news. The tree was dying. A passing tree surgeon engaged us in conversation. He pointed to some of the upper branches and said he had seen these symptoms before, and that our tree was in trouble.

We called in a second opinion. A company dedicated to the preservation of large trees confirmed the doctor's analysis, and suggested intravenous feedings. One of the workers explained that our area had suffered through a drought twenty years ago. Some of the trees had experienced trauma and the effects were just beginning to show.

He prescribed a series of intravenous feedings. They inserted a dozen needles with packets of nutrients attached. His assistant told me that I should also try talking to the tree.

"Trees are like any other living thing," she said. "They're happier when you pay attention to them." She had a lovely, open face which turned slightly as she spoke, like a flower towards sunlight.

I sat on the raised roots with my nine year old daughter and a book in my hand. I was more willing to be seen reading aloud to a child than to be thought by passersby to be talking to a tree.

I even considered buying a headset for my cell phone and pretending to be engaged in long phone conversations when I would really be sharing my thoughts with the tree on the state of the world.

Despite the feedings and the readings, we were soon informed that though the tree might look healthy, it could fall at any moment, doing harm to the house or anyone unfortunate enough to be walking by.

We didn't want to be there when the tree came down, so we planned its disappearance for our vacation week. We returned to find only the stump, wide and flat, like a table without legs.

"At least we still have the stump," I said next morning, but by the time I arrived home from work it had been ground into woodchips.

I went to sit on one of the swings, finding in the sudden absence of the tree its overwhelming presence.

My wife thought we should take the swing set down. "No one uses it anymore," she said.

Twenty yards from where I sat, beyond the picket fence, lived our new neighbors, a young couple. I could hear an infant crying.

We had thought the house would be diminished by the loss of the tree, but it emerged as if from a shadow. People asked if we'd had it painted or made some other change.

The young couple stopped to talk to us. They introduced us to Daisy, who sat in her stroller like a queen. They were flush with the newness of parenthood, the truest of loves.

"When she's ready," I heard myself say, "come by and use the swing set."

Next, I was showing it to them, like a tour guide. Although the wood was weathered, it had really never looked better, especially underfoot where I had filled the frame evenly with fresh woodchips from the beech tree.

Playoff

Someone had scratched out part of the letter "N" in the word "NO" on the sign at the entrance to the park; instead of "No Dogs Allowed," it read "10 Dogs Allowed."

Maybe that explained why there were two dogs nosing around behind the backstop. A silver cat watched them from her regal perch atop the stone wall.

It was the beginning of the end of the summer. The traveling baseball teams that had played well enough were still in the game. On this particular night two of those teams would meet each other in a playoff, and the winners' summer would continue just a little bit longer than the losers'.

The players' mothers and the siblings took their seats in the metallic stands. The fathers would trickle in as the evening proceeded, in shirt sleeves or suit coats, some carrying briefcases. The younger brothers and sisters of the players clearly did not grasp the importance of the moment. The older sisters found their friends, and from the rhythm of their speech, you could tell that they were happy to be here, but you also got the feeling that their noisy exuberance might have nothing to do with the game about to be played.

The home team was just finishing its warm-ups. The umpire whisked off the plate and rose to his full height, looking through the backstop at the seated fans. He had the physique of a player himself. He turned around, shouted "Play ball!" and put on his mask, getting down to business.

The first batter drove the second pitch of the game deep into center field where the outfielder planted himself under it and made the catch. With only two pitches thrown, the tempo had been set, and every spectator who had endured the season could see why these two teams of thirteen year olds had made it this far. Their play was several cuts above that of their contemporaries.

Every parent hung on every pitch, except for one woman. She was deeply absorbed in reading a book.

She had long, blond hair that hid her face from a side view. She was slim, had a summer tan, and wore a yellow, sleeveless top and blue jean shorts. I had never seen her before.

I ran through the list of players to try to determine whose mother she could possibly be. It made sense that someone too busy to attend any of the season's games might show up now that the team was fighting for a championship. But it didn't make sense that she would display such disinterest. I imagined her son begging her to come, and she complying technically, without ever looking up from her book.

It was a hard cover book that looked to be well over 500 pages long. She had read a little more than half of it. She seemed totally absorbed in every sentence. She had it open on one knee, the other leg sometimes dangling down to the next row, sometimes pairing itself up so her two knees touched.

I decided that I had to do two things: see her face and find out what book she was reading.

I leaned as far as I dared from my seat two rows up from hers. The title was repeated at the top of every right-hand page. From where I sat I could see the word "After ..." but no more.

By now two innings had ended and the game was scoreless. Both pitchers were right on the money, and the play behind them had been sparkling.

I thought I saw the word "the" after "After." "After the ..."

The ping of the bat and the sudden bursts of cheers from everyone sitting all around her did not make her raise her head. Neither did the barking and snarling of the two dogs who had somehow managed to cross each other after an hour of harmony. They were only ten feet from her and yet she still did not look up from her book.

I made my way down the stands and walked over to the water fountain, so that I could come back and glance at her face. The home team scored on a triple followed by a sacrifice fly. This brought the hometown crowd to its feet twice, with high-fives and backslapping, except for her. She remained seated and turned the next page.

She was a good-looking woman, with regular features and a fresh complexion. Maybe she was an aunt visiting for the day. Or maybe a baby-sitter for one of the younger siblings. No, a baby-sitter would have looked up at least once or twice to make sure that her charge was still in the park. How could anyone be so neutral?

Why would anyone so uninvolved in the game choose to sit here to read her book? There were so many more attractive benches throughout the town in less noisy, more secluded spots. There were the benches around the pond where the only sound was the occasional quack from a duck. Why not sit there? I began to feel sorry for the player she had come to see, whoever that was.

After seven innings the score was tied at 2. The game went into extra innings. Pending darkness arrived to influence the outcome. In the bottom of the second extra inning, the home team rallied, putting together three straight singles and winning the game on a dramatic play at the plate which sent dirt flying in all directions. The umpire gestured and loudly pronounced the runner safe. The winning team ran on the field to embrace the batter and congratulate themselves. The fans cheered and clapped. Only the woman reading the book didn't look up.

We all went off to our cars, some with light steps and smiling faces, and others looking dejected and dragging their feet. I drove down the narrow road past the umpire who had his trunk wide open. He had just removed his chest protector when she came up, threw her arms around him, and they kissed warmly. He was still holding the mask, but she had dropped her book so that it fell into the street with the pages open.

Her Idea

It was her idea.

My nine-year old daughter decided that she and I should take a walk around the block with the dog each evening, right at 8 o'clock.

She was very exact about this as she is about everything.

We began these walks in the fall. When we would leave house it was already getting dark; by the time we returned, it was night.

During one walk, she announced: "I'm going to count the stars."

"How can you do that?"

"Why can't I?" she asked.

"There are too many of them," I said, and we both looked up at the night sky to see how countable the stars seemed.

"It would be like trying to count all of these leaves," I said. The sidewalks were littered with leaves. Sometimes, we were walking in them, ankle-deep. The dog nosed through them. He had no interest in anything above his head. I tried to remember if I had ever seen the dog look at the sky.

"Besides," I said, "some of those stars aren't there any more."

"What do you mean?" she said.

"Some of them are so far away that it takes a really long time for the light that they send out to reach our eyes. Sometimes it takes so long that even though they've disappeared the light is still reaching our eyes, so we think they're still there."

"I don't understand."

"Everything we see gives off an image that travels to our eyes through the light. Even that tree," I said. We were stopped at the corner, under the streetlamp at a tree the dog had chosen to sniff.

"You mean that tree isn't really there?" she asked.

"No," I said. "That tree is definitely there. But it's so close that we see it right away. But some things are so far away that we think they're still there when they're not."

"You mean like memories?"

"Yeah," I said, "like memories," and while I said it I saw her transform before my eyes into a young woman in her twenties, in her thirties, simple and elegant, exact and compassionate.

And I knew with certainty that this moment, under the streetlamp, would have a future as one of my memories.

The Alumni Game

This will be a bittersweet year for the high school baseball team. The team is full of promise. Six of the starting varsity players are seniors who have been playing at this level since their sophomore year. There is more and better pitching this year than in any we can remember. This year everything points to a winning season.

Most of the seniors also played football. That this was their last football season seemed to take them unaware until the final few games, but that experience has informed this one, and they go into this baseball season not only knowing, but also feeling from the start that this will be the last time they play together.

The feeling extends beyond the field into the stands. The six seniors are the only boys in their families. Six fathers, passionate and well meaning fans, also go into their final season.

It was with these thoughts in mind that I arrived early for the annual alumni game, which opens the season. In this game, alumni, recent and not so recent, play the current high school squad. Usually, the alumni play their hearts out. For the high school team, this game is their first chance to air out their arms and practice their strokes in preparation for the coming season; for the alumni, this game is their season.

I am not an alumnus of our town's high school, so I could hardly expect to play, but I just happened to have my glove and my spikes in the car. So when it seemed as if the alumni team might not have enough players, I just happened to be standing there. After happily agreeing to fill in, I walked slowly to the car but my heart was leaping at the prospect of stepping onto the field again.

I played third base. You might consider the hot corner, where a line drive can be on you in an instant, a dangerous choice for someone "slightly" out of practice. I think of third base as pure instinct. And instincts stay with you, no matter what.

I played through my youth as a shortstop, where instinct is also important, of course, but range is really the thing. Over the shoulder catches in the outfield, hard ground balls hit deep into the hole, longer throws, stolen bases, pivots and double plays—by contrast, third base is a quiet place, a house in the country, an alligator dozing in the heat, ready to snap without notice.

My only concern was the bunt. But when I looked at the kids, swinging the bat for the first time after the long winter, I felt sure that no one had bunting in mind.

I took my position and with it came some razzing from the fans, my friends. "What are you going to do," the third-base coach said, "if he hits it your way?" He was referring to my son, who had just stepped into the batter's box.

"Throw him out," I said. "Just like anyone else."

He took the first pitch for a strike. He took the next two for balls. Each time I touched the ground with my glove—easier to come up than go down—ready for a line drive or a bouncing ball that might come my way, no matter how hard.

Instead, he stroked the next pitch deep into right center field, an ever-increasing arc, high over the heads of the scrambling outfielders, much farther than I could have ever hit a ball. As he rounded the bases, I found myself clapping, drawing the attention of my teammates. He passed me in a hurry, touching all four bases well ahead of the throw.

Suddenly, I understood. We were playing the alumni game. As parents, we played it every day. With every pitch we hoped they would hit the ball farther than we ever could. And if we were there to see it, the reward would be even greater.

Trampoline

The beginning of the year is birthday season for us. We have three children, one born in January, one in February, and one in March. Our younger daughter's birthday is the last day of March.

This year, we fulfilled one of her long-time wishes by getting her a trampoline. It was too large to bring into the house, so we put it in the garage, and covered the box with two over-sized party bags.

On the birthday morning, we all got up early and shared an elaborate breakfast—French toast, scrambled eggs, fresh strawberries, three kinds of juices. When all of the gifts had been opened, she thanked everyone again. She seemed content, even though the usual, one, large gift had not materialized.

Then my wife said, "We have your big gift for you. It's out on the driveway."

She looked at us with all of the amazement an eleven-year old could summon, and blurted out, "You bought me a car!"

A car, of course, is the ultimate trampoline. Our son got his car from his cousin—a white 1995 Mustang in need of a paint job. It disappears into the stratosphere and returns to home base with the regularity of a teenager's erratic schedule.

We plan to replace the swing set in the backyard with the trampoline. When the refrigerator repairman told us about his two children by marriage and the three children he and his wife had adopted, we offered him the swing set. His children are still young enough to thrill at first flight.

As if it had happened this morning, I remember swinging each of our kids on that set. The swings are attached to the wooden bar above by a series of chain links. In time, I remember showing each child how to pump, and re-discovering with each of them the joys of self-propulsion.

My job is to get the swing set down and the trampoline up before summer. There are no links of any kind in the trampoline box, no moving parts. The kids will be the moving parts, bouncing between the pulls of desire and gravity.

By end of summer, our 18-year old son will find his wings, leaving home to attend college in another city. My wife has already marked the family calendar. He will fly back to us five times during the school year touching down for the briefest of stays.

Witness

Here's how it is sometimes when you live in a small town, even when it exists in the shadow of a great metropolitan center.

I was in the middle of my Saturday morning errands. I check the mail at my office which is in the same town where I live. If the mail gives me a reason to walk over to the bank I always do so in the best of moods.

On occasion, I will go from the bank to the post office, but this is rare on Saturdays, since the short hours usually mean long lines. Better to leave the post office for a weekday.

Often, I go to the library, which takes me back to within 50 yards of my office. All three of these buildings are within walking distance. I can see the other two from each of them. With the latest internet developments, the library has truly transformed into a doorway to the world. It's possible now to go online, request a book or film from virtually anywhere in the state and have it arrive in two days. This awesome capability almost guarantees my weekly visit.

As I left the bank, I saw a dog standing just outside the door, so close, in fact, that I had to open it carefully in order not to hit him. How irresponsible, I thought, to leave your dog outside while you went to the bank without even tying him up, and on closer look, without tags of any kind. The dog was good looking, but somewhat thin, with unsettlingly blue eyes. As I walked away he followed me.

I crossed the street in the direction of my car and he followed close behind. I now realized that his owner must not be inside the bank. Upon reaching the other side of the street, he chose to trail a couple pushing a baby stroller, and I got into my car.

I drove for about 80 yards, and made a U-turn as usual, pointing the car in the direction of my house. This would not be a library day. There were too many other things to do. When I reached the major intersection, I saw the dog in the middle of the street, looking lost, with cars passing on either side of him. I pulled over and quickly got out. I held my hand up to stop the traffic, walked over to him, and coaxed him out of the street and onto the sidewalk.

People walking in both directions stopped. A moment later, a police car arrived. I knew the officer; he played left field on my softball team.

"This yours?" he asked.

"No," I said.

"Some lady flagged me down," he offered.

"That dog walked all the way from the car wash," one of the passersby said. For a human, it would not have been such a long walk, but for a dog in traffic it seemed like an act of hopeless desperation.

"Anybody got a leash?" Bobby, the officer, asked. "Or anything we could use for one?"

I put my hands on the roof of my car and looked into the back where I had a sports bag with a detachable strap I thought might serve the purpose.

"I think I have something," I said. Bobby looked over my shoulder as I peered into the car.

At this exact moment, my 11-year old daughter's friend and her mother drove through the intersection. The girl had a new cell phone she had just gotten for her birthday which she used to call my daughter who in turn called my wife.

The sports bag reminded me that we had a game the next day.

"You coming tomorrow?" I asked Bobby, as I handed him the strap.

"I'll be there," he said, fashioning a perfect leash. Clearly, he had done this before.

"I'll bring this back to you," he said, gesturing towards the strap, which was now loosely, but securely in place around the dog's neck. He led him into the patrol car.

I was home minutes later. I found my wife waiting for me in the kitchen.

"What happened with the police?" she asked, in a weary tone. "Several people called me. Your daughter's friend said they made you put your hands against the car and that they were interrogating you."

Flight Plan

My wife warned me not to go to my office.

"You'll get all caught up in something," she said, "and we'll never get on the road. It happens every time."

"No, I won't," I said. "I'm just going to print out the directions. It'll take two seconds. We can't go without them."

My office is less than a mile from my house. I parked out front and ran up the flight of stairs to the second floor.

I quickly sat at one of the computers. The digital clock on the desk read 7:30AM. Plenty of time. We were on our way to visit our son, newly at college. It was what I called "Parents' Invasion Weekend." The university would get the chance to show us what we were paying for and my wife would get the chance to see how he was doing without her cooking.

I typed in the destination and clicked on the print button. The output was barely readable. The cartridge in the laser printer was nearly out of ink. I knew I could squeeze a few more days out of it by shaking the cartridge. I came away with black streaks of toner on my hands.

I clicked on the button again and the directions printed—not crisp, but legible. Happy that only a few minutes had passed, I locked the door which still held my keys. Past experience had taught me to keep them there on really short visits; otherwise, I might lose precious moments wildly searching for where I possibly could have put them down.

As the key turned in the lock, I decided to wash the toner off my hands before getting back to the car. The bathroom was a small, white room only ten steps down the hallway. When I opened the door, I was surprised to find it occupied.

The window was open on the bottom by nearly a foot. In the overlap between the top part of the bottom half of the window and the bottom part of the fixed upper half, a bird struggled to get free.

After taking a step back in surprise, I went closer to it. The one eye I could see seemed to be looking back at me. The bird rested, then put up a ferocious fight, then rested again, then put up another ferocious fight. I could see that at least one of his legs was caught beneath the window's lock. Clearly, he had flown in through the open window and in attempting to fly back out fallen into this unwitting trap.

I looked at my watch. The easiest thing would have been to simply shut the door and leave.

Maybe I could inform someone before leaving who would help. The police station was across the street. I could just imagine myself filing a report about a bird stuck in a bathroom. I'd never hear the end of it.

I looked at my watch again. Maybe I could get him free somehow. The closer I got to the window, the more the situation unnerved me. The bird looked scared and desperate in his accidental cage; it was weird to get so close to so unwilling a creature, but it had to be even weirder for him.

I thought about trying to raise the window, but that would only further entrap him. I thought about lowering the window but even if that freed him, where would he go inside the closed bathroom. Even more important, how could I get the window up or down without wrecking the legs that he couldn't get free.

Something else concerned me. Once I got him free, how frenetic would his actions be?

Would he attack out of desperation?

I went back to my office and took the pair of sunglasses from my desk. I also looked around for a pole or something else with some length that would allow me to jiggle the window from a distance. I came back into the bathroom, looking like a 21st century jouster without his mount.

The pole didn't work. I walked up to the window and rattled it from side to side. The bird's eye kept looking at me. He struggled with everything he had and when he rested in between struggles he seemed to despair. But then he would struggle again. I kept trying to push the window in any direction. If it moved it did so minimally. Ten minutes must have passed.

Then, suddenly, he flew up and out.

I moved to the door. He skirted along the ceiling with a great fluttering. Seeing the blue sky through the window, he repeatedly flew directly into the glass at the very top, trying to find the secret way out. He flew directly into the glass a dozen times.

Now, it was getting late. The window was still open a foot wide at the bottom. He flew wildly around the room and crashed into the glass again. There was a wide sill under the open window. I had done as much as I could, especially with the time pressure. He had come in through the open window; in time, I felt sure he would find the way out. After thrashing around long enough, he'd probably come to rest on the window sill and feel the stream of air from the outside world.

When I got home, household items and foodstuffs intended for our son were stacked up awaiting transport. Our two daughters were waiting, each wearing earplugs to her own iPod.

"Don't even tell me what happened," my wife said.

"Nothing happened," I said. "Here are the directions."

On the way down, she asked me how she thought my son would feel about her offering to clean his room.

"I don't think it's a good idea," I said.

We spent a very pleasant day together. We missed him greatly, and we let him know it, but we also took pleasure in his newfound freedom.

After I dropped the family back at our house, I went back to my office. I had images of finding the bird dead on the floor, or in the waste basket where the cleaning service which sometimes worked on the weekends might have put it. Or I thought I might find it quiet in the room, philosophical by now, still unable to find its way out.

The light was streaming from under the closed door. I opened it cautiously. My eye went to the corners of the ceiling. The night was black through the glass. A cold breeze chilled the room.

The bird had flown.

The Presentation

Finally, the price had come down. For several years, we had wanted a portable projector for the company so that we could make presentations on the road without depending on the in-house facilities of our prospects. But the cost was just too high, especially for equipment that would be carried from place to place, endure cab rides, train rides, and airplane trips, and possibly even get lost.

Two things put us over the edge. The price dropped significantly and a new type of screen appeared on the market, which could be opened side to side to the desirable width, and stand on its own on a table or desk.

Once we made the decision to buy, there was a mad rush to close the deal. We had an important meeting scheduled and the screen turned out to be not that easy to find. It had to be bought from a dealer and none of them kept it in stock. We learned that the item would have to be assembled by the manufacturer, and that this would only happen after the order had been placed. Then it had to be sent to the dealer. Then the dealer would send it to us.

Having made the decision, the purchase became indispensable to us. The harder it became to get, the more critical it seemed. The shorter the time between its possible appearance and the moment of our scheduled departure for the meeting, the more integral it became to our success. The presentation itself also grew in stature. When the chance of receiving the equipment in time seemed impossibly remote, the presentation loomed as the most important one we would ever make.

Then comedy prevailed. Where we could not find a dealer before, we were soon contacted by several dealers at once. For an anxious few hours, it seemed as if we would end up with two of everything, a travel version and one that would stay in the office, wiping out the savings that had motivated us.

In the nick of time, it all worked out. The equipment arrived the day before we needed it. The digital picture it gave was sharp and lifelike. The screen was sleek and professional. I carefully packed the projector and screen in the back of the car.

It was my mother's birthday. Because she had reached an important number, her four children and their families decided that we should celebrate with a surprise dinner in a restaurant near her home. Underline the word surprise. My parents never went to restaurants. I mean never. My mother, who is the world's greatest cook, always said: "Why go to a restaurant? Food is better at home."

If she was cooking the meal, we agreed. It would be useless to point out that there are other reasons for going to a restaurant than the food. These reasons would have made no sense to her, since the only atmosphere she really approved of was her own house and the people she favored most in the world were the members of her own family.

If we had held the celebration in one of our houses, she would never have sat still for it. She would have gotten deeply involved in cooking, serving, and cleaning up, making sure everyone had exactly what they needed. She would have made a dish for my father, for the younger grandchildren, and for anyone else who seemed to be without.

But this was exactly what we did not want, especially at a meal in her honor. For some time now, we had been arranging ways to see my parents without tiring them out, especially my mother. My father, so active during our youth, did not try to do anything anymore. He was nearly immobile. Getting him into the car was a major ordeal. For eight years now, my mother had taken complete care of him. She was tired, and we could see it. But she would not listen to any of our pleas to get help inside the house. The very idea of an outsider intruding on her space, even with the best of intentions, was anathema to her.

"I'll do it until I can't do it anymore," she said.

So you might understand why the only way we could get her to a restaurant was to make it a surprise. She and my father thought they were on the way to my sister's house where we would all meet them. We chose my nephew, the most believable member of the family, to pick up Mom and Dad. Under the pretense of having to give something to a friend who owned a boat, he drove into the marina near the restaurant.

We met the car. Mom was surprised. She called us all liars, affectionately. I explained that my brother, her second son, had really wanted to be there, but could not make the trip from California. She said she understood. Then when she saw him sitting at the table, she called us all liars again.

There were fifteen of us at the dinner. We had a great time. All of the kids seemed to have digital cameras and picture phones they were testing out, so there are dozens of photographs, posed and candid shots, from many different angles, like the unconscious memories of an ordinary day.

My sister asked me to say a few words. I had nothing planned. At a quiet moment, I raised my glass, and said: "This is for Mom who taught us everything we know about goodness, and beauty, and hope. Thanks, Mom. We owe it all to you." Her face brightened. Uncharacteristically, she let the focus rest upon her for the briefest moment, and I felt that she was grateful for us and this celebration.

The phone call came about seven o'clock the next morning.

My brother reported in a tired, unbelieving tone that Mom had cried out in the night in terrible pain. He had carried her down the stairs. He had followed the ambulance in his rented car. My sister had arrived with her husband to meet them in the emergency room. They had waited seven hours while the emergency room doctors tried to determine what was wrong. They couldn't give her pain killers, they said, because they didn't know what was wrong. Now the surgeon had arrived, taken one look, and announced that there was not a minute to lose. They had to operate. It was a matter of life and death. My brother was calling to let us know. With the phone in my hand, I began to dress quickly so I could make the drive back.

My wife came with me. I had been in this situation before. There was a three-hour ride ahead, and I did not feel right listening to music or the banter of talk radio. I asked her if she would mind listening to a collection of CD's I had taken from the library, all about the 20th century, the "American Century." I put in the CD about the 20's, the decade in which both of my parents had been born, prelude to the Depression, in which they had grown up. Then, the War Years. My mother would lose a brother. My father would enter the European theater. On the last day of the war, the man sitting next to him would be killed by a sniper, a bullet my father would always feel had been intended for him, the only officer in the group.

My mother lay there under many tubes, with a breathing apparatus over her face. The surgeon had informed us that he did not expect her to last 24 hours, but she did. She lived for 23 days in the Intensive Care Unit—a blur of days for us, in which she was conscious but could not really speak. She could roll her eyes, and smile when I said, "Mom, get better! We need stuffed shells!"

After these 23 days, she moved to a hospital room and then four days later she was brought to a rehabilitation facility, where she would regain her strength so we could take her home. But she did not regain her strength. She wasn't eating. She couldn't keep food down.

We begged her to try to eat. She seemed depressed. We were so unused to seeing her this way that we did not know what to do. I didn't want disappointment or puzzlement to show on my face. I walked out to the parking lot, while my sister stayed behind. I was trying to come to terms with something, but I did not know exactly what it was. I leaned against the car. I looked inside at the clothes I had been storing there for what had become long stretches of time away from home.

I took out the projector and the screen, in its hard case. My laptop computer was on the front seat. For months now, whenever I visited my parents on the farm which they owned, I would go out on the land with my digital camera and take pictures of my mother's flowers, of the different structures and statues, the antique farm implements. I captured the wide expanse of the land, and all of the carefully arranged plantings. The trees had a dignity all their own. The house itself was silent and beautiful. So was the barn. Everything was as my mother and father had always wanted it. Even though they did not appear in any of these pictures, they were present everywhere in them.

I walked back into the building shouldering my equipment, like an infantryman. Once in the room, I opened the screen and put it on the table against the wall. I positioned the projector so the image would be large and clear. I turned on the laptop and watched the picture form—the front of the house, which Mom so loved, and had not seen for a month now. Miraculously, she brightened. As the pictures advanced—her flowers, her trees, all nine grandchildren sitting together on the porch, the chicken coop she had turned into a walk-in dollhouse for the kids—she actually reached for the cup of juice and drank it. For a moment, she seemed happy again.

Over the next few days, we took turns showing the pictures. Each time, Mom brightened and drank and ate. It made us happy and hopeful. As I walked back to the car at the end of visiting hours, it struck me that I had never even attended the meetings for which the equipment had been so hurriedly purchased, and that the all important presentation for which I had prepared was this one, taking place against the cream-colored wall.

On New Years Eve, I felt comfortable enough to go home, for the first time in ten days. I had dinner with friends. By 10 AM the next morning, I was in the car rushing back to the hospital. Mom had been brought back to the emergency room.

We surrounded her and held her hands and whispered encouragement. My father sat in a wheelchair, wearing a Yankees hat and looking confused. It was too much for him. Even at this dire moment, Mom rallied again. She was soon in a hospital room and the doctor reported that her vital signs were improving.

Throughout the day, she improved while we prepared to bring her home. I wanted to know from the doctors whether she would know she was home. They could not answer us definitively. I knew what they thought bringing her home meant, but to us we all felt in our hearts that once she was back at the farm, surrounded by her things, the things she had made with her own hands, the things that she loved, she would rally again.

They must have known what we felt, so they suggested that we wait to see whether another day would make her even stronger. We slept in the hospital that night, all four of her children, on any chair or couch we could find.

During the next day, she continued to improve. The morning became the afternoon, and soon the sky outside the window began to darken. Since she seemed to be getting better, I suggested that we split the hours of the night between us. It wasn't necessary that everyone be there, only that someone be there at all times. In the morning, they would be taking her home. It was all arranged.

Everyone drove off to change clothes, take a shower, to return phone calls. I stayed behind with Mom. I sat at the head of the bed, while she lay there with her eyes closed, breathing evenly. In the quiet of the room, I could only think all the way back to when our positions had been reversed, and she had sat alongside my childhood bed and read me stories and poems. I called my brother on the cell phone and asked him to bring back "The Tin Soldier," and "The Land of Counterpane," a poem by Robert Louis Stevenson about a boy who lay sick in bed. They were what first came to mind when I remembered her reading to me. I told him exactly where he would find them at the farm. She had carefully arranged a permanent bedroom for each family, and put in it the things of each of our youths.

While I waited for him to return, I held her hand and talked about bringing her home. I wanted to read to her, but I had nothing except the loose pages that might one day be collected into this book. I read the story about the star shower, with the dog and the night. I read about the stuffed animal that my daughter loved so much. I read about my son and his mother and aunt, the question they asked, and the amusing answers he gave. There were stories I knew she liked. And then I read the last story in this book, finishing with the last sentence, which so completely expressed how she felt about life and the world.

My brother returned. We talked about bringing Mom home in the morning, and how we would re-arrange the room. I said I hoped that we could position her bed so that she would see the light coming in through the window. We were relieved that her breathing had become less labored. At different times, we had had different goals, but all we could think about now was seeing her back at the house.

Then her breathing changed. Suddenly it had a different sound. I hurried out to the nursing station and asked someone to please come to the bed. "Her breathing sounds different," I said.

"That's what happens," one of the nurses said.

She walked past me into the room. She moved the pillow slightly, but did nothing else.

I dialed my sister's cell phone. She lived forty-five minutes away. She had not arrived home yet. My brother-in-law turned the car around and headed back to the hospital. "Don't get in an accident," I said, "but hurry."

I called my father and told him what was happening. I could hear him sigh into the phone, and I knew that he would not be up to the car trip to the hospital, the elevator ride to the third floor, or even the lonely passage in the wheelchair down the corridor.

My younger sister arrived. All four of us and my brother-in-law stood close to the bed. We took turns, two at a time, one on each hand, thanking her, whispering, saying good-bye without saying the word.

Our fiercest hopes kept adjusting. We were like negotiators without a penny to deal. Moments ago we had bargained for six months, then three months, now we would have joyously embraced another day, even another hour.

When her breathing stopped, I realized that until that moment I had never experienced the end of anything.

Then we were encompassed by something we knew would never end, beginning within us, no more than a pin-prick, and spreading rapidly to fill the entire universe—this unutterable loneliness for one person—sudden, intense, unquenchable.

The 16th Character

We would have preferred to bury my mother in the small cemetery next to the church where she had chosen to worship. With its uneven rows of crosses and crooked headstones, this small stretch of land on the side of the road seemed more approachable than the military cemetery where my father had earned a place for himself and his spouse.

You have ten days from internment to submit an epitaph. You are permitted two lines of no more than 15 characters each, including spaces.

After thinking for a day, I suggested these words to my brother and sisters:

A life of beauty
and goodness

Everyone agreed that this phrase expressed her physical beauty, her sense of style, her talent for creating beauty with everything she did—the garden, the house, the clothing, the paintings, the cooking—her goodness to others.

The receptionist at the military cemetery, while sympathetic about my loss, informed me that there were sixteen characters in the first line.

"What will they do about that?" I asked.

"They'll just leave off the last one."

Of course that wouldn't work. I promised to call back.

Through the day I tried to rearrange the words. I looked for substitute words. I counted characters, over and over. I shared the dilemma with my siblings, and they shared it with their children. We all tried to come up with a new set of words that would say as much as the one we were forbidden to use.

But nothing worked. That original phrase took on the status of an incomparable painting that we had seen once only. We could not find another to match it.

I called the military cemetery again. I gave the name and number. The woman on the phone remembered me, which was encouraging. I said that we had tried very hard to find a replacement phrase but that there was nothing we liked as much.

There was a pause. I realized that she did not know what I was talking about, and then I began to wonder whether she actually did remember me, or if she had perfected a way of letting people feel that she remembered them, especially if they announced in the first few words that they had called before.

But as quickly as this thought formed, it was forced out of my mind by my determination to try to save the words.

"Is there any way," I said, "that we could change the size of the font so that all of the words would fit?"

"No," she said.

"But characters have different sizes. Maybe this set of characters will fit?"

"We make them all the same size."

In desperation, I said: "Maybe we could combine two words that everyone would recognize as separate like *ALife* and then we'd have only fifteen characters.

"We wouldn't allow that," she said.

"Listen, I said, this was a very special person who was always there for everybody, and never did anything halfway, if you knew her or even saw her once you'd make an exception."

In the most understanding tone of voice she could summon, she said, "There are no exceptions. The 16th character must be a space."

I hung up the phone and walked outside into the January weather. It was cold and the wind blew the tattered remnants of leaves in circles before dropping them to the ground. I was angry and I was thankful. I was thankful to the voice on the phone for making it so clear that whatever words we chose they would be followed by a space, and that it was a space we would never fill.

Heart Attack

My daughter surprised me. When I announced that I would be taking the long trip to see my father in the hospital, she offered to come with me.

This was the same nine-year old girl who had asked me earlier in the year, "Is Grandpa mad because he's old?"

"No," I had answered back then. "He was that way when he was younger, too." But how much younger, I wondered. I would have to remember to ask the remaining aunts and uncles.

In return for her generosity, I was determined to make the ride as pleasurable as possible. I set her up in the back seat with the laptop and her Sims CD, so that she could play the game for the full three-hour drive if she wished. I pulled over on the Cross Bronx Expressway when she complained that glare was preventing her from seeing the screen. I closed my jacket in the window so it stayed in place like a curtain, blocking the sun.

When we got there, he was propped up in the bed, eyes open. This was encouraging. Other times, he slept through the entire visit. I wanted him to see that she had come, and I wanted her to be able to see him awake, too.

"Dad," I said, and he turned slowly towards me. "Look who came to see you?"

"Oh," he said when his eyes met hers, and he smiled. He had once seemed like the handsomest man in the world. Now he was grizzled and toothless on one side; his blue eyes were sunken and distant-looking. She stepped forward to kiss him. He said, "I love you."

"I love you, Grandpa," she said. I sat there in silence, stunned by her bravery and the naturalness of her actions. If my own life were to leave me at that moment my last image would have been one of unimaginable purity.

I set up the framed picture I had taken last week. It showed him in his hospital bed surrounded by four barbershop singers from the chapter he had belonged to years ago. Almost from the moment my mother left us, he had begun to sing a song, "When I Lost You," with very sad lyrics. It gave me the idea to contact the barbershop chapter to see if anyone remembered him.

When the spokesman assured me that he knew my father, I asked a favor. Could they get together a quartet to visit him in the hospital and sing a few songs? Two days later they appeared like four guardian angels. For the first time since the death of my mother, he smiled and had actual conversations. He inquired after certain members of the group. He wanted to know what the theme of this year's chapter show would be.

One of the men answered: "Love. We're still romantics."

"I know," my father said, in a slurred voice.

He sang along with them through every number. At the end, they cheered, and assured him: "You still have it."

Luckily, I had my digital camera with me and I caught it all in short movies the length of each song and snapshots, posed and candid. I had to show them to get anyone who had visited him in recent weeks to believe that anything like what I described had taken place.

It struck me that there may be a moment looming ahead for each of us in which those who surround us will power down their expectations drastically, a moment when a smile or a question or an interaction of any kind will earn the status of a major achievement.

When I had the picture positioned so that he could see it without turning his head, the private investigator tapped me on the shoulder and motioned towards the door. I had heard about this man, but never met him.

"What's going on?' he asked. "I didn't know your father was here. I saw his name on the patient list."

He handed me a card that said *Private Investigations*, and told me that he farmed a little patch of land next to my parents' house, where he grew flowers and vegetables.

"I'm on a job here," he added. "Tracking some guy's wife."

I could tell from what he was not saying that he didn't know my mother had died. I broke it to him slowly. He was shocked by the news. He watched someone walk down the hallway and said he had to leave, but would come back for sure to look in on my father.

"Such a lovely woman," he turned to say. "I can't believe she's gone."

When I returned to the room my daughter was sitting quietly in the chair, and my father was sleeping.

"Do you feel ready to go?" I asked her.

She nodded yes.

Today was a good day. He smiled. He seemed happy. We owed it all to her.

"Bye, Dad," I said, and kissed his forehead while he slept. It was warm with life, in sharp, ironic contrast with my mother's forehead when I last placed my lips upon it. I thought about the grief we had caused each other, as old and as inevitable as fathers and sons. I would not see him alive again.

We walked through the lobby, passing the private investigator sitting against the wall, pretending to read a newspaper. I held her hand tightly and thought that no matter how long I lived I would never be able to make her understand what a gift she had given this day. She had attacked my heart and left it limp.

"I'm going to get you something," I said, as we got in the car, "for coming today and making Grandpa so happy."

She picked out a crafts store, and once inside the store, she selected two unpainted bird houses. We would work on them together.

"Grandpa likes birds," she reminded me.

"I think he likes them because they sing," I said, "and he likes to sing."

He had once found a bird with an injured wing at his doorstep and nursed it back to health, until it could fly again on its own. It was good memory to end this day.

Tire Tracks

The ambulance had left the deepest tire tracks. Then the day before the funeral, the farmer who lived on the adjacent plot came by with his plow and cleared away the snow. He did this without looking up, or making even the slightest gesture, as if he were merely fulfilling an unspoken tradition.

His work left the ground wet. When the guests came back to the house, they parked in all directions. More tire tracks.

In the ensuing days, the ground hardened and softened again just enough that the four children, now orphans, each took a rake in hand and tried together to remove the ruts and return the ground to its smooth state, where the grass could grow evenly again.

One of the rakes was only half a rake. It only had teeth on one side. No doubt, my father had saved it because it was still useful. He may have actually rescued it from somewhere, maybe the dump, which he visited regularly to throw things away, but often returned with things that other people had thrown away, much to my mother's chagrin.

One day, without his consent, she hired a dumpster, and with my sister as assistant and eventually referee, she began to load it with all of the superfluous items she could find. As she filled the dumpster, he emptied it, squirreling away things that he felt he could not live without. Discussions that could be called arguments broke out. It would have made a great one-act play. Astute critics would have noted that despite the laughter in the theater, the action was really about love, desire, and the longing for immortality.

Later, when he had become virtually immobile, spending his days in a favorite chair on the ground floor, facing the television and the stairway, my mother slowly cleared out the basement, where he had saved unimaginable things in the most organized fashion. He had plastic boxes on shelf after shelf of screws and nuts, separated by size. He had cartons of bent nails that he must have planned to straighten one day. He had tremendous balls of aluminum foil and bits of string tied together and wrapped around stick after stick of wood. He had identical unidentifiable objects, thousands of them in boxes together—what looked like broken parts of electrical devices. He had scrap paper stacked evenly, with typing on one side only—saved from his work days and even his college days—some pages well over fifty years old.

"Why does he save this stuff?" my mother would ask. The answer only occurred to me now, as I swung the rake at the deeper ridges. It was a mutual relationship he had with these things he saved. He extended their lives and the notion that they would all in time become useful to him held out the promise of many days to come.

My mother saved things, too. She seemed to have every toy we had ever played with, many in their original boxes. Her photo albums were more complete and more organized than those of anyone else on the planet. Each picture had the date and a description written on the back. The albums filled the walls. She had spent several months of the last year of her life transforming what had once been a chicken coop into a dollhouse. In it, she had placed the playthings of our youth for the grandchildren to see and touch—trains, dolls, animals, soldiers, tea sets, games of all kinds.

The best approach was to attack the highest ridges with the rake's prongs, loosening the dirt so it fell into the valleys, smoothing it over with the same gesture. This would have been easier work in summer, or even spring, but with winter so recent, the earth resisted. An hour's progress showed little.

It was amazing that the house still stood. They had put so much of themselves into it and the surrounding acres that we just could not conceive of it continuing to exist without them. We were reluctant to move anything. We could not accept that they were gone. This was something more physical than a thought. Deep down, we knew we would never see them or talk to them again, and this was a kind of knowing that made us feel as if we had never known anything before. They would never have let these tire tracks mar the landscape, so we had to make them disappear as completely as possible, or accept the unacceptable.

I saw the ruts as deep wounds. I heard the two surgeons, a mere sixty days apart, telling us in almost exactly the same words, that there was not a minute to lose, that there was no option but to open the patient up. The rake was an extension of my arms; the tines were my ten fingers. Slowly, but desperately, I wanted to close these wounds, to make everything whole again.

The music on the cassette player came through the open window. It seemed foreign and new, yet understandable in a way it had not been before. Moving through the air, it transported emotion; it was made of the stuff. It welled from the inside out.

Across the street lived a composer, his wife, and their young daughter. I learned that they had visited my parents often, that my mother had thrown a first birthday party for the little girl and invited all of the neighbors. This was years before my father became ill. It gave me a warm feeling. It reduced the impression I had of their separateness and isolation in this country house.

Suddenly it seemed that the only way to capture their lives would be to write a symphony with clashing cymbals and enormous sounds with hundreds of violins and quiet pizzicato solos. I would drop my rake right now and run across the street, knock on the composer's door and explain the necessity. Surely, he would understand. We'd stay up all night, several nights in a row, whatever it took, until the work was done, until it expressed all the beauty and tragedy that makes up a life, never mind that I knew nothing about music.

On the last day of World War II, my father posed with his men for a celebratory photo. A German sniper shot and killed the man sitting next to him. Being the only officer in the group, he lived the rest of his life certain that the bullet had been intended for him. That sniper's bullet struck again 50 years later in the form of leukemia. It left him badly wounded, but he survived. The third bullet, the death of my mother, he could not resist. On the morning of the day he was scheduled to leave the hospital, the nursing staff reported that he was *unarousable,* a word I had never heard.

All afternoon, the breeze carried the voices from the cassette player to our ears. They were singing about love, and heartache, and sunny days just around the corner. The big band sound faded in and out.

It was impossible to erase all of the impressions. The ground was too unforgiving. I stared into the deepest ruts and saw only blankness.

When we had done as much as we felt we could do, we got the buckets of grass seed from the barn, where our parents had left them, and spread the seeds liberally wherever the earth was cut, in the hope that new grass would grow.

Insomnia

My daughter can't sleep. When I ask her why, she says she doesn't know and starts to cry.

It is a week since my father's funeral.

When she is under the covers again, I pull the rocking chair up to the side of the bed. She knows I won't leave until she is safely asleep.

The dog is lying in the corner of the room. She thought that having him there would help her to sleep, but it hasn't worked. Before this experiment, he had never climbed any stairs in the house, either up or down. I could only conclude that somewhere in his past, before we rescued him, something had happened to him on a stairway.

Harmless re-runs show on the television, with the volume turned down low. She thought that having a television would help her sleep, but it hasn't worked. I get up and turn off the TV.

I cannot rock without thinking. I cannot think without recounting the day.

For weeks, I had avoided taking any trips. My sisters, who lived nearby, went to see him every day. I made the trip of 100 miles each way as often as I could, at least twice a week. Sometimes, he slept through the entire visit. Each day since my mother's passing, he had seemed to deteriorate further. But then, things began to look up. On the day scheduled to discuss his discharge from the hospital, I felt it was safe to take a long-delayed trip to Washington. I e-mailed my questions for the doctors so my sisters could add them to their own. I drove south.

Two hours into my meeting the calls began to come. My sister announced that Dad had been brought to the emergency room. I checked flight schedules. I called a cab. I scheduled a flight. I reserved a rental car.

Inside the airport, I felt curiously empty-handed. I suddenly realized that I never went anywhere without carrying something. Here I was in the airport, buying a one-way ticket in an incredible rush and carrying no luggage, not even a laptop bag.

Once through security, having been checked and questioned, I felt empty. I could not imagine just sitting on the plane, however short the trip might be. I headed for the bookstore.

I heard two people animatedly discussing a novel. The man was recommending the book to the woman. "It's the best I've read in years," he said. I had heard of it, too. I picked it up. I liked how it felt. It was a paperback that filled my hand. It felt substantial.

I had one of those flashes—comforting and unsettling at once. So that's how it is with me and books, I thought. I turn to a book like a friend. Confronted with life, I turn to a book.

Alternately, I read a few pages, and looked out the window. The narrator told me about his youth in a faraway place. The voice was full of regret and realization, no doubt foreshadowing events to come later in the story. I looked out the window and felt the blankness.

The blankness had to do with my father. It was a feeling of nothingness we had between us. It was nobody's fault. It was our fault.

When the plane landed, I made my way quickly to the rental car counter. While I waited for the paperwork to be put before me, my cell phone rang. It was my brother-in-law. He told me Dad had not made it.

Now the blankness hit me all in a rush. That he died when I was not there fed the blankness. I left the counter and went up the escalator in search of the subway, walking slowly. There was no need to drive out to the house on the island now. I could do that tomorrow. Instead, I would take the subway to the city, and then the train to my town. It would be a long ride. I wanted it to be a long ride.

As I rocked, I thought about some of my last conversations with my mother, about how tired she seemed. How intent, despite her tiredness, she was to clear the basement of the farmhouse of all the things she considered useless that he had categorized and saved.

To make her point, she handed me a jar full of rubber washers of various thicknesses.

Now what stuck me was the accumulation of a life, of matters large and small, and how much it seemed not to matter at all, how the life vanished. Later I would learn that in those last moments, he tried to say something. He repeated the same sounds twice to one of my sisters who put her head to his ear; and then again to the other sister, the same unintelligible sounds. What was he trying to say?

The dog rustled in the corner. He rose and walked around the room. He couldn't sleep either. The sound of his metal tags clinked as he walked and my daughter awoke from the sleep she had finally achieved.

"I'll take off his collar," I said, "so it doesn't make noise."

"No," she said. "What if he runs away?"

I knew she wouldn't sleep worrying about the collar, so I left it on, and it continued to rattle metallically whenever he moved. Her eyes were wide open again.

"Let's go downstairs," I said. We went down to the basement where the tools are kept. I was looking for something, but I didn't know what, when I saw the jar of rubber washers.

Back upstairs, we picked out washers of just the right thickness and size and placed them in between the dog's three metal tags so that when the collar moved, they made no sound.

Soon she was fast asleep.

Act of God

The farmer who lived next door to my parents' recent home called me at work. He had bad news. One of the trees had fallen and damaged the roof of the barn.

"But that tree was healthy," I asked. "Wasn't it?"

"We had some heavy winds," he said. "They're calling it an act of God."

"Who is?"

"The insurance company," he said. "The agent came by. He lives down the road. He knew your parents."

There was a pause.

"I just wanted you to know that because they're calling it an act of God, they're saying that they're not responsible."

There was another pause while I tried to imagine so rooted and healthy a tree lying against the barn.

"And you do have to get it moved," he said, "because the longer it's there the more damage it will do."

I knew that my parents and the farmer exchanged helpful information like this all the time. I thanked him and called my sisters who already knew that the tree had come down. They knew because one of my mother's friends, the landscapist, had called. This woman had admired my mother's garden, her work ethic, her sense of style, her way with living things.

She told me about all of this on the day my mother was buried. We took a walk together in the garden. There was snow on the ground. We talked about the flowers that were not yet in bloom, and how they would fare without my mother to tend them. We talked about the trees which stood there in their bare elegance.

The trees had presence. They gave you the feeling that they had always been there, and that they would continue to be there forever.

We took another walk like this, sixty days later, on the day of my father's funeral. She told me how much she admired my parents, how often she had passed them working in the field, and what a good feeling it gave her. This was all before my father became too sick to leave the house. Then she told me that she was in awe of how completely my mother took care of him, and then how surprised she was, like the rest of us, that my mother, the healthy one, went first. "That's how I want to go," she said, speaking of my father, "right after my loved one."

One day, three weeks since the tree had hit the barn, I picked up the ringing phone to hear her voice on the other end.

"I need to tell you that a second tree fell," she said. "This time it's the sick one that has been losing its leaves. Now that I see it down," the landscapist in her said, "I'm really surprised that it stood for this long."

There is a Season

From the trunk of the car I took the usual items and one more: glove, bat, new ball still in the box, scorebook, and this time, the digital camera. This was our first playoff game and possibly our last game of the season, and I wanted a picture of the team that almost wasn't.

The team had been in existence for 20 years. I had played ever since we moved to the town, thirteen years ago. Never once in all that time had we come close to forfeiting a game, but this year, at the outset, it just did not seem like we had enough players to field a team. Injured knees and family obligations had depleted our numbers. This was the over-thirty league, and most of us were in our forties.

At the last minute, we appealed to the town police. Four officers wanted to play. They explained that they alternated shifts on Sundays and that we could expect to see two of them each week. On the day of the first game, two passersby in the park expressed interest in playing. One was an urban type, wearing dark glasses with his ear almost always glued to a cell phone. The other looked bookish; even though he stood there in sweats and a baseball hat, you imagined him wearing a suit and a striped tie. He explained to us how much he liked the sport, that he had talented voice, that he sometimes sang the star spangled banner for the local minor league team. It was an uneven collection of players that grew into a team and finished the regular season with a respectable record. After all here we were, about to enter the playoffs.

During batting practice I went to third base where I knew I would play this game. On a sleepy Sunday morning, third base in slow-pitch softball is an efficient place to rapidly wake up. It was more like tennis than baseball. I'm proud to say that nothing got by me, in the practice or the game.

Coming off the field, I quickly decided that trying to take the picture before the game would be a mistake. We needed every ounce of concentration we could summon for the contest; besides, the act of taking the photo would seem to imply that I felt that we would not survive the single elimination to take the photo next week. I'd wait until the end of the game.

We went down in order in the top of the first inning. They scored twice in the bottom of the inning. In the top of the second, our fifth batter doubled. I was batting sixth. Years ago, I had concentrated on the art of hitting the ball to any field; it was the defensive strategy of a spray hitter without much power. I surveyed the field from my position in the batter's box and decided that right-center field would give me the best opportunity to drop in a single and score the runner. I hit the ball exactly where I wanted it to go, but instead of falling in front of the outfielder, it took off and soared over his head. As I rounded first base, I saw his back as he ran after the ball. As I approached the third base coach, he was actually waving me home. No one in the entire park was more astonished than me. I crossed the plate with the first home run of my career and the score was tied.

Hitting a homerun is different. No matter how much you may think or say a hit is a hit and getting on base is all that matters, a homerun feels different. It is the perfect harmony of bat, ball and swing; it feels entirely smooth and connected, like something that was meant to be, maybe like all things that are meant to be. It feels like winning the Oscar, compared to consoling yourself with the thought that it's all politics, and no one can recognize true art.

The game see sawed. They went ahead 4-2. We went ahead 6-4. I got a second hit, a single this time. They tied it at 6. Then, in what would become their last atbat, they shot ahead with 8 runs. It was nobody's fault; it was just how softball scoring went. After trying to eke out a walk, I made the first out of our last inning with a fly ball to center field.

I asked the captain of the other team to take our picture. Everyone lined up. He pointed and clicked, but nothing happened. He tried again. "Is the battery dead," he asked. Regardless, I knew the moment was passed; I couldn't get them to pose again; a loss made everyone want to leave the field in a hurry.

We all shook hands and congratulated each other on a great season. I gathered up the same items I had carried from the car before the game, except for the ball, and walked back to the parking lot. There I saw two of our players talking to an elderly man. As I approached, they addressed me.

"He's looking for a field," one of the guys said, "where his grandson played last week. He thought it was here, but it isn't. He says there were several fields together."

"A lot of fields," the old man said.

"Brookdale," I suggested.

"Yeah, Brookdale," they agreed. It was somewhat out of the way—the largest park in the area, with a track, soccer fields, at least five softball fields, even a dog run."

"How do I get there?" the old man asked.

They both began to give him directions, and I saw a bewildered look come over his face.

"I can take you there," I said.

"Okay," he answered. "I'll follow you."

We had about three miles to cover. I took him through many streets, checking every so often to make sure I hadn't lost him. I stopped at every yellow light. When we finally entered the secluded expanse of the park with its tremendous trees and colorful bicyclists, I pulled over and he dutifully came to a stop behind me. Even before he lowered the window, I could see him shaking his head no.

"This is not it," he said.

"Are you sure?" I asked. "There are several fields just around the bend."

"No," he nodded. "I don't recognize anything."

"Then where could it possibly be," I wondered, aloud, and then I asked, "How old is your grandson?"

I thought the image of 12 or 15-year olds might make the connection for me.

"It's my son I've come to see," he corrected me. "He has a make-up double-header because the field was too wet to play last week. I can't believe how late I am."

"How old is your son?" I asked.

"My son is sixty-six years old."

He must be in his late eighties, I thought. Maybe he's ninety. It moved me that he had driven out to see his sixty-six year old boy's double-header, and how anxious he was about missing the beginning.

"It starts at 10 o'clock," he said.

"Does your son have a cell phone?" I asked. "I could call him."

He nodded no.

"What about calling his house? Maybe his wife has the schedule."

"I can't remember the number. I can't remember anything," he said, in a regretful voice.

"Are you sure it was this week?" I asked. "It didn't rain last week. It rained the week before. The field was wet when we played two weeks ago. Are you sure the double-header is this week?"

"I'm sure," he said, and then, "I don't want to take up any more of your day. You've got things to do."

"It's okay," I said. If we found the game, I was now considering watching an inning or two. Maybe it was an over-sixty league.

He mentioned a certain road and asked me to take him back there. From there, he would drive to his son's house and ask his daughter-in-law if she knew where the games were being played. "Although I doubt it," he added.

I walked back to the car and led him through the streets in the direction he wanted to go. After a mile or two, I pulled over again with the thought of asking him one or two more questions, but he assumed I had arrived at my destination and waved to me as he drove by.

"Good luck," I said as he slowly moved out of sight, but in a voice that only I could hear, and suddenly it struck me that I did not have a father anymore.

Inexplicably, the lens of the digital camera zoomed out. So it does work, I thought. Next year, I'll check the battery.

Cloud Cover

Because I had described the last star shower in such vivid detail, the children decided that they wanted to be waked up for this one. It seemed odd to me that another of these once-in-a-lifetime events would take place so quickly after the summer show. The newspapers had reported that this light display would not be equaled for another ninety-nine years.

I got up at 5:00AM, and went down to put on the coffee. Minutes later, I heard the sound of small feet overhead. I wondered how she, at seven years old, had managed to rise on time without the help of an alarm clock.

I had planned to make sure that the sky was spectacular enough before waking anyone. Now, here she was, already dressed; so out we went with the dog. For him, there is no wrong time escape the house.

"Do you make a wish before you see the star," she asked, "or when you see it?"

"You keep the wish in your mind," I answered, "and then you make it as soon as you see the star."

The sky was almost gray. This worried me. I couldn't tell whether the grayness meant cloud cover, which the newscasts had warned might hide everything. Then we saw a star shoot briefly across the lower part of the sky.

"Did you see it?" I said.

She hadn't seen it, but my report was enough for her to run excitedly into the house and up the stairs to get her sister. The show paused for them both to come back, the older one rubbing her eyes, and feeling the cold.

We three looked up, but we saw nothing. And then we saw another.

"I saw that one," my older daughter announced. "It's cold out here." She went into the house for a blanket, and returned with it draped around her shoulders.

She stuck it out for another five minutes, then let us know that she was going back to bed.

The summer shower had offered so much more.

"Did you make a wish, Daddy?"

"Yes, I did." I wished for a replay of the summer for her.

"If we both make a wish for the same star," she asked, "will it work?"

"Sure it will," I said. "Think about how many people there are in the world looking up and making a wish on the same star?" According to the newspaper accounts, whatever event we would see tonight had actually happened in 1866. What had become of the wishes of all of those contemporaries?

In the end, I saw only five shooting stars, and my daughter said she had seen seven. She added our counts together, even though we had been watching the same stars, and summarized the evening by crediting us with twelve sightings.

"That's a lot," she said, in a satisfied voice. "I'm tired." I brought her in the house, and then came back out to get the dog.

By now, the sun was rising. Behind the branches of the leafless winter trees, a delicate mix of colors painted the sky: rose, apricot, magenta. Why did we need the extraordinary, when each morning brought us wonders like this?

978-0-595-44059-7
0-595-44059-2